Access Denied

A true story written by
David E. Gates

Copyright © 2013, David E. Gates

All rights reserved. No part of this book may be reproduced, stored, or transmitted by any means - whether auditory, graphic, mechanical, or electronic -without written permission of both publisher and author.
Unauthorised reproduction of any part of this work is illegal and is punishable by law.

ISBN-13: 978-1503242241
ISBN-10: 1503242242

Dedication:

For Julie
For Shelley
For my Mum

Special Thanks to:

NACSA - National Association for Child Support Action
(www.nacsa.co.uk)
Maura and Jeremy Crawley
Deb Hallett
James Holmes
Graham Wheatley

This book is based on true events.
Some names and identifying details have been changed to protect the privacy of individuals.

To Marion,

I'm humbled by your response to my book.

Thank you.

Love,

David L. Gutz
-x-

Chapter One

I had been working at Oracle, the second largest computer database company in the world, for about seven years when I first met Meg.

Oracle's offices were in Bracknell, based within the ring-road known as "The Ring." Housed in a brown-coloured, hideously square, block-styled and rather drab building, I worked as a Shift Leader of a team of computer operators in the company's I.T. department for about five years before moving into the role of Media Team Manager within their customer support organisation.

The Shift Leader role had been one that involved working shifts, as the name implies, and the new Media Team manager position meant that I now worked regular office hours, from nine-to-five or thereabouts.

The new role was much better because it meant I had a social life once more and could interact with people during the day. I ran the small but vital department from a small area in the offices on the ground floor.

One morning, I went to the in-house gym on the top floor of the Oracle building to weigh myself. My weight was somewhat over what it should be, as usual, and I was on yet *another* diet and checking my progress.

When I got to the gym, I found the scales to be absent. I returned to the ground floor and went to the Reception area where the security guard, Dave, advised me the scales had been used in the call-centre by the receptionists.

Dave took me around to the call-centre area and we entered to retrieve the scales. Inside the room were the receptionists who took it in turns to be on the phones and to man the reception desk in the main atrium of the building. My attention was drawn to a girl at the far side of the room, blonde, pretty and smiling.

I saw the scales at the foot of the table and retrieved them stating I would return them to the gym. The girls, all busy on calls, smiled and nodded their "hellos" and "goodbye's."

When Dave and I exited the room, a tall, leggy blonde came past.

Dave said "Hello" to her and, as we moved along the corridor, Dave gave me a nudge.

"I'd do some damage to that," He said. "Wouldn't you?"

"Not really my type, if I'm honest." I replied.

"What? You're joking?" Dave proclaimed. I was, but felt she was somewhat out of my league.

"I tend to go more for that type in the corner." I said, nodding towards the pretty girl with blonde hair.

"Meg?" Dave asked.

"I don't know what her name is, but yeah the one on the far side in the corner." I said.

"Meg." Dave confirmed. "I'll see what I can do." Dave said. I rolled my eyes as, knowing Dave as I did, I thought he would be crude and therefore ruin any chance I had with her.

"Well, don't push it. Just find out if she's seeing anyone." I said.

"Leave it with me." Dave said.

I returned the scales to the gym. I stepped on the scales and convinced myself by leaning this way and that that I'd lost some weight but knew for sure it would be put on again sometime soon and no amount of leaning or lifting my feet up would make any difference.

* * *

Later that day, whenever I had an opportunity to walk across the atrium, I'd look across at the main reception desk. Meg was there on one occasion and I nearly walked into a huge plant that decorated the lobby area as I looked over at her. She smiled back sweetly and I became somewhat embarrassed and hastily walked through to the offices back to my desk.

Shortly after I returned to my desk, my phone rang. It was one of the older and more "gossipy" women from the call centre, Lydia. It was obvious Lydia and the other girls were having some fun at the fact that Dave had gone into the room shortly after I'd left and announced that "Someone was interested in Meg."

It hadn't taken the girls long to work out who of course. I grimaced.

"When you going to ask her out then?" Lydia laughed.

"Who said I was?" I replied.

"Well, you nearly walked into the tree in the atrium because you couldn't take your eyes off her." She countered. I could hear laughing in the background. My embarrassment trebled.

"Well, I don't know. I mean, I know nothing about her." I said.

"If you ask her, you can find out all you need to know." Lydia teased.

"We'll see." I said. I was keen not to make a spectacle of myself or be the subject of someone else's amusement. Last thing I wanted was to be the subject of gossip.

"Well, I'll tell her you fancy her if you don't ask her out." She warned.

* * *

Over the next few hours, whenever I was in the computer room, the windows of which faced into the atrium, I could see the girls in the call-centre room smiling, laughing and waving at me. Once they were sure I'd seen them, they'd point at Meg on reception and then at me, signalling us "together" by intertwining their little fingers on each hand.

I decided that there was nothing for it but to ask her out. What did I have to lose apart from a little dignity?

I went back to my desk. From there I was able to see the reception area. I picked up the phone and dialled the main front desk. Meg answered. She had a nice voice.

"Hi. I don't know if you remember me from this morning, when I came in to get the scales, but I wondered if you fancied going for a drink sometime." I blurted out.

"Sure." She answered coolly.

For some reason, I never expected her to agree to go out with me. I guess I was out of practice in respect of asking girls out – usually you just met in a pub, chatted, snogged then progressed from there. When she agreed, I was totally unprepared.

"Err, okay. Err, well, when, er, and where?" I stammered.

"I don't mind. Next week?" She offered.

We agreed on a date the following week and I said I'd pick her up.

* * *

Over the next couple of days, I found out it was Meg's birthday. Exactly three weeks after mine. A number of "18" balloons were hanging around her chair. I sent her a card and felt quite pleased with myself that a girl twelve years my junior was happy to go on a date with me. Not that she knew how old I was at this time of course.

The women in the call-centre were delighted in the "union". They teased me at every opportunity and constantly stated that they thought we would make a "good couple."

Meg lived with her parents and her brother in Bracknell in an area called Birch Hill. Her sister, Faye, lived with her boyfriend just a few doors away.

I arrived in good time to pick her up and met her mother, a large, imposing but very friendly woman and her father who seemed not much older than I was.

We left the house and I drove us through Great Windsor Park towards the town of Windsor itself. We parked up and walked along the river to a small, quiet pub.

We had a couple of drinks, chatted and got on surprisingly well.

On the way back to her house, I somehow managed to take a wrong turn and had to pull into a dark lane to execute a U-turn. Meg joked at how I was "driving her down dark lanes," especially considering that I "hardly knew her."

I parked at the same point I had when I collected her and we agreed we'd go out again. She left the car and her mother would comment to her later how surprised she was I hadn't tried for a kiss.

I was a gentleman after all.

Chapter Two

Over the next few weeks, I saw Meg regularly. We would drink in her local pub, called The Silver Birch, which she'd been a regular of since she was about fourteen years old.

We were falling in love with each other and grew closer and closer as time went on. The age difference hadn't bothered me. If anything, I felt somewhat privileged to be thirty years old and dating a girl twelve years younger. Not many men my age dated women that young.

I was due to travel with work to the United States to see how their operation was run and exchange knowledge on practices which worked best for each of our departments.

A day or so before, when I was at her parent's house, Meg called me into her bedroom and said she had something to tell me. We sat down on the edge of her bed. Meg rummaged through a file and pulled out a document. She passed it to me. It was her birth certificate. I looked it over briefly and couldn't find anything obviously amiss and looked at her quizzically.

"What?" I said.

"Don't you see?" Meg responded.

"No." I looked again. I couldn't see anything. "What am I looking for?"

"Look at the date of birth." She said, directing me to the part of the document which noted when she was born.

"And?" I said, still somewhat perplexed as to what I was looking for.

"The year." She said. I looked closer.

"Nineteen-seventy-nine?" I asked. "So?"

"Well?" She asked. And waited.

"I still don't get it. What?" I said.

"I'm not eighteen. I'm seventeen." Meg said, putting me out of my mathematical misery. I smiled.

"So?" I asked.

"You're not bothered?"

"No. Why would I be?" I said. "Truth be told, I'm even more chuffed."

It appeared that someone in the receptionist's area had assumed it was Meg's eighteenth birthday and Meg hadn't corrected them. Once the balloon and cards arrived she felt it was something she couldn't resolve with them.

Meg hugged me and told me she wanted to tell me before I went to America in case it changed things between us. I hugged her back and told her she was daft.

* * *

Meg ended up spending more and more time with me, as we became closer and continued to fall for each other.

Frequent evenings and almost every weekend we'd be together.

At weekends, we'd invariably be at my home in Portsmouth. The first night I took Meg there, I was anxious about our sleeping arrangements. Meg was a confident woman and she took the lead somewhat regarding this and said she'd be sleeping in the same bed as me.

We spent the evening at a friend's birthday bash, where Meg was to meet a number of my close friends; Sean, Adam, Greg and several others.

After this, we spent the weekend mostly in bed.

* * *

Whilst our relationship was good, Meg's jealousy was something I was to witness first-hand on the first New Year's Eve that we spent together. We agreed to go to Shamus O'Donnell's – an Irish themed pub which most of my friends gravitated to, to bring in the New Year. We all got on very well with the landlord and his wife and having a lock-in was the norm. That was one of the main attractions of going there as, before licensing hours were extended, most pubs chucked out at eleven o'clock at night.

When the chimes of Big Ben echoed throughout the pub via the television or radio, everyone moved around the pub hugging and kissing each other.

I can be something of a flirt at times and when it came to my moving around the pub, and finding myself kissing the rather attractive barmaid, Meg's jealousy came to the fore. She blew up and made it clear that my enjoyment of celebrating with the barmaid was overstepping the mark. Feeling I'd done nothing wrong, I disagreed with Meg. We argued. I could have understood it if I'd had my tongue down the barmaid's throat, but I hadn't.

I ended up leaving the pub and then walking away from Meg as she continued to argue with me in the street. I hate arguing in public and felt it best just to go home.

I got home and waited for Meg to turn up. By the time I went to bed, she still hadn't come home and I got a text message saying she was staying over at Adam's house. I wasn't altogether surprised. Adam and Meg got on very well together and it was clear he'd looked out for her when I'd gone home and left her there.

Meg turned up the next day, wearing one of Adam's t-shirts which made me initially suspicious that something had gone on between them. I was assured nothing had and it wasn't long before we made up.

Friends would later come to describe my relationship with Meg as "turbulent", "up and down" and "on and off".

We broke up several times in the first couple of years. I didn't attribute this to any particular party's fault. The age gap may have had an influence to some degree but I don't remember being aware of this being an issue per se whilst we were together. I think that we just wanted different things from the relationship.

Even when we'd split up, during late 1998, we were still sleeping together and spending evenings together from time to time.

So, when Meg phoned me in early February of 1999 to tell me she was pregnant, I was a bit tactless to say the least. We hadn't been together properly for a while though had continued to sleep together. I still remember the first thing I said to her when she told me she was pregnant:

"Is it mine?" I asked.

"Of course it's yours, David." Meg said.

Chapter Three

My house in Portsmouth was on the market within a few weeks of finding out I was going to be a dad. I was elated. I'd always wanted kids and now it was going to become a reality. I had wanted to move to a better place for some time and this gave me the perfect excuse to do so.

I wanted kids for two reasons. First was that I always wanted to be a dad. I love kids and doted on my sister's and my friends' kids. Secondly, and of much less importance, my family name dies with me. Of course, I'd need a son to carry on my family name, but that was something I didn't have a lot of control over. Either way, I was ecstatic about the prospect of becoming a father.

Meg and I agreed we wouldn't tell anyone, except very close family, about the impending birth until the three month scan had been completed so that we knew we were past the point when most miscarriages and other problems during early pregnancy occur.

My mum was overjoyed at the news. Both my sisters had their kids already and I suppose my mother always thought, considering I was the oldest, that I'd be the first to settle and have kids.

My house sold in April 1999 and I spent the next couple of months sleeping between my mum's, my friend's and Meg's parents' whilst we looked for a new house together.

In May, after a relatively short search, we found a house in Segensworth, near Fareham in Hampshire. It was everything I'd wanted in a home.

My last abode was somewhat old and run-down and required a lot of work to keep it up to a reasonable standard. The new house, plot 11, Jacaranda Close, was brand new. I'd always liked the idea of having a brand new house.

Whilst the estate it was on wasn't quite finished, we managed to get a good deal where the property developer paid our 5% deposit for us if we were willing to move in whilst the area was still partially a building site.

I wanted to buy the house under my name only but my income and debt at the time meant that we needed Meg's salary to ensure getting the full amount we needed for the mortgage to complete the purchase. I agonised over this for some time.

Having been tied into a house with a previous girlfriend and suffered the grief and costs associated with taking it over when we'd split up, I was reluctant to go down that route again. Whilst, at the time, I thought Meg and I would be together forever, I just didn't want to run the risk of history repeating itself. I eventually had to relent when it became clear this was the only option if we were to buy a home for ourselves and our soon-to-be family.

We moved in during the summer.

We bought everything, except my television, hi-fi equipment and office furniture, new. It was a lovely house made even better once the sofa, beds and other furniture and curtains were put up and blinds installed.

The garden looked out over a small wooded copse which housed a variety of wildlife including squirrels that frequented the nut housings I set up around the garden. Ever since seeing squirrels in the garden of a friend's house, I'd had a dream of having the same creatures visit my own garden. The dream was starting to come true.

The neighbours were nice too. James, next door, was a movie and PlayStation nut like me and we hit it off immediately. The other neighbours kept themselves to themselves but we'd hit gold in respect of location and quiet.

Meg set about decorating the nursery with Walt Disney Winnie-the-Pooh decals along the wall at waist height and matching curtains and lamp shades with the same Disney theme. Everything was coming together. We gradually bought the furniture for our new-born's room. Mostly neutral, pine furniture. We bought a cot, chest of drawers and other accessories required for a baby's bedroom.

We were even arguing less. We had just one argument during the whole five months we were in the house before the baby was born.

Everything was set. Now we just had to wait.

* * *

Dean, my long-time friend since secondary school days, had a girlfriend called Karen who was studying to be a nurse. As a result, Karen had spent time in various hospitals around the south of England and asked us which hospital we were going to.

We told Karen that we'd been allocated to the Royal Berkshire Hospital in Slough despite there being two hospitals, one in Ascot and the other in Frimley, that were much closer to where Meg lived at her parents'. The Ascot based one didn't deal with pregnancies so that limited our choice but Karen told us that Frimley was "really nice, especially compared to the Royal Berkshire."

Meg arranged to change hospitals and attended Frimley hospital when she was about three months' pregnant to have the first ultrasound scan. Unfortunately, I couldn't attend as I was in America on business but phoned Meg as soon as I could after she'd had the scan.

Apparently it had all gone very well and there were no complications or worries highlighted. Meg was so excited when I phoned to see how it went.

"It's amazing," She exclaimed. "You can see the arms and legs and head and everything."

Meg went on to tell me how she'd gotten an extra copy of the still picture of the scan for me.

When I returned from the States, she gave it to me. When I saw it, I was amazed at the detail that could be seen. The shape of the head, the back and the legs were clearly visible on the fuzzy black and white image. Nothing was going to stop me from attending the second scan.

As everything looked good from the initial ultrasound session, we began to tell more people our news.

* * *

The second scan, about twenty weeks into the pregnancy, was even more amazing. We attended Frimley hospital and entered the sonographer's room where the scanning equipment was.

Meg laid on the bed and lifted her top up to reveal her belly. I held her hand as a nurse poured some gel onto her stomach and then positioned the scanning tool, known as a transducer, against her tummy moving it slowly and smoothly over the entire area.

As the nurse moved the transducer we could see the skeleton outline showing the bones of the spine and hands of our baby on the monitor screen. During one moment the baby opened and closed its left hand.

"The baby's saying 'Hello'." The nurse said.

I said "Hello" back towards Meg's belly and was genuinely moved and started welling up a little as I made first contact with my unborn child. The connection had been made and I now started feeling a part of something bigger and better than anything I'd ever been a part of before.

Nothing untoward was announced during the second scan and I proudly showed everyone the scan picture. I simply couldn't wait and felt so chuffed that it was going to happen. I was going to be a dad.

* * *

Towards the end of the pregnancy, Meg started spending time at her parents. She'd become bored at the house in Fareham due to a lack of local friends, a situation she'd not really taken the opportunity to improve. Most of the time she'd spent watching daytime TV without getting out and meeting others in her situation. The few friends Meg had met since moving to Fareham either made scant effort to visit or Meg failed to invite them over.

I was still commuting to the office on a daily basis and as I drove up the M3 motorway, I received a call from Meg. She was clearly panicked and tearful and told me that the baby hadn't moved that morning. Meg had gotten used to being woken up by the baby's morning movements and having the routine broken caused her to worry somewhat.

I tried to calm her down, telling her to ring the doctor to check. My eyes welled up at the thought of losing the baby and I struggled to keep my composure and remain calm for Meg's sake. Meg explained she had been in touch with the doctor who'd told her to contact the hospital. The hospital, in turn, had told her to go in so they could check everything was okay.

I diverted from the M3 along the A31 towards Farnham and on to Frimley. As I drove, I prayed that everything would be alright. I parked up and ran into the hospital. I found Meg in a room full of other expectant mothers. She had a gadget strapped to her waist. It was a heart monitor and it listened and played out the baby's heartbeat which was quick but consistent.

The nurse and Meg explained that baby was probably just having a lie-in that morning and that's why there had been no movements. Everything was good. The relief was immense. I took Meg home before going on to work and prayed that nothing would go wrong in the last few weeks.

* * *

The baby was due around the first or second week of November 1999. Everything was ready for the new arrival and there'd been no further scares or worries during the weeks leading up to the expected birth date. Everyone was excited.

Two weeks past the due date and our baby still hadn't arrived by a natural course of events. Meg was instructed to go into the hospital to be induced. We attended the hospital on a Sunday evening and Meg was prepped and given inducement drugs. I stayed as long as I was allowed but had to leave once it was clear nothing was going to happen that evening.

After twenty-four hours, there were no signs of dilation and Meg was given further doses of the inducement medicine to try and expedite the birth but this had, seemingly, no effect in prompting the birth either.

Yet another day passed and there were still no movements or signs that the baby was going to come out on its own volition.

Meg was exhausted. The hospital ward she was in was noisy due to other mums either making noise through discomfort or from sounds of impending births. As a result, she'd barely slept over the last three days and was totally exhausted.

The next morning, Wednesday, Meg was taken for another scan. Everything was okay and the mid-wife said that no further inducement drugs could be administered as Meg had already had the maximum dosage over the last few days and she'd have to wait for at least another day before she could begin the course of drugs again.

We were told there were two options: Wait until the course of drugs could begin again and hope the baby makes an appearance in the meantime or have a caesarean birth.

We asked the mid-wife what her recommendation would be. She explained that as a nurse and mid-wife she was an advocate of natural births and recommended these whenever possible. Sensing her professional stance on the predicament we were in, I asked her what she would do if it was her that was due to give birth in exactly the same situation. She went on to explain that the placenta, the "food and nourishment" resource for the baby whilst it's in the womb, was drying out. It had been more than two weeks since the baby was due after all and this was not unexpected but the further the placenta dried out then the bigger risk there was to the baby. I pushed her to speak "off-the-record".

"If it was me lying there, I'd go for the caesarean." She said.

We spoke with the doctor and explained we wanted a little time to discuss the options and, most of all, Meg wanted to spend a night in her own bed so she could rest properly ahead of the birth seeing as she'd barely had any sleep in the last few days.

The doctor agreed this was okay but told us we had to make a decision before the next morning.

We returned to Meg's parents and determined, for the sake of both mother and baby, that the caesarean was probably the best course of action if nothing happened before our return to the hospital the next day.

Meg enjoyed a long relaxing bath and a good night's sleep in her own bed.

* * *

On Thursday, 25th November, we returned to the hospital shortly after lunchtime. Nothing had happened overnight and we decided to progress with a caesarean birth. It wasn't our preferred option but in the absence of the baby making any movement to come out of its comfort zone, it seemed to be our only choice.

We had to wait for some time before the theatre was available and then we were "smocked-up" in operations theatre clothing. I was dressed in a blue "robe" and hat whilst Meg wore a white all-in-one loose-fitting gown.

Just after 3.00 PM, we were led into the theatre. Meg was anxious and I held her hand trying to keep her calm.

Two doctors and two nurses were present. Meg was to be given an epidural to counter the pain she'd experience during the operation and the doctor opened Meg's gown at her back and started using his fingers to count down the vertebrae in her spine to determine where to insert the long, thick needle to administer the anaesthetic. He was having some difficulty locating exactly the right spot and urged Meg to remain still and calm. Feeling it was my cue to try and relax Meg, I tried to take her mind off the situation.

"Just think, you'll be able to have some cheesecake when this is all over." I said. Cheesecake was Meg's favourite dessert and during the pregnancy she'd not been permitted to have any.

Meg laughed and the doctor frowned and again reminded her to keep as still as possible. My eyes widened with guilt at the faux pas I'd made.

The needle finally went in and Meg, clearly in some pain, gripped my hands so hard the end of my fingers whitened as the fluid from the syringe was pumped into her spine.

After a few moments, Meg was laid on her back and one of the nurses put up a small "screen" over Meg's belly, hiding the area where the doctor would operate from our view.

I continued to hold Meg's left hand as I was positioned on a stool beside the gurney.

The doctors raised Meg's gown over her belly and began the operation. Despite my curiosity and macabre interest in all things of blood and gore, I felt unable to bring myself to look over the screen to see the intricacies of the operation that was happening right before us.

Meg had relaxed and within what seemed to be no time at all, the doctors had performed the caesarean and the baby was brought out of the womb. Held for a moment just high enough for us to see, the bloodied form was cradled by a nurse and taken to the far side of the operating theatre. We were told it was a baby girl and I told Meg that I hadn't known what to expect but that the sight of our little girl was "the most beautiful thing I'd ever seen." I wept, as I am now recalling this here, and kissed Meg as we waited for the baby to be cleaned and passed to us.

Within a few moments the baby, having been cleaned and weighed – a whopping ten pounds five ounces! – was passed to me. Meg's prone state made her unable to sit up as the doctors continued to complete the operation by sewing her belly back together.

I held the little form in my arms and showed her to Meg. We both cried.

The nurse took a photo with the camera I'd brought in, and told me that if I put my little finger in the baby's mouth, she'd suckle on it. Normally, the baby would be passed straight to the mother to bring it to the breast quickly but due to the operation this wasn't possible. I did as the nurse instructed and instantly bonded with the baby that was our new daughter.

The operation was eventually finished and Meg was able to hold our new-born. We were placed in a room just off the ward where Meg had spent several sleepless nights.

A different mid-wife gave Meg instruction on breast-feeding which she attempted and continued with despite great discomfort. The baby fed well and, despite the pain Meg was feeling, she persevered to breast-feed (and would do so over the next two weeks) to ensure the baby received all the nutrients and anti-bodies that are so important for good health and immunity during the formative years.

We spent the next few hours together as a new family and started to think of and discuss various names for our new offspring. Had it been a boy, it would have been easy we each agreed, but a baby girl was something that we'd given scant attention to of in terms of providing a name.

The end of visiting time came quicker than expected and I was forced to leave Meg and our baby together in the hospital. Far from being upset to do so, I saw it as a chance for them to bond and for me to tell everyone.

Once I was immediately out of the hospital building, I phoned my parents, Meg's parents, and several of my friends. I truly couldn't believe I was a dad and the action of telling each and every one that I phoned brought tears to my eyes every time.

I arranged to have a quick drink with Chris [Butch], a friend from work. I spent the time excitedly telling him everything that had happened over the last few days. It had culminated in being the best experience of my life to date. After a couple of drinks, I returned to Meg's parents and, exhausted, fell asleep a very happy and elated "Dad".

* * *

Family members and friends came to see the baby whilst we remained at the hospital over the next couple of days. We still didn't have a name. Suggestions came and went but nothing seemed to fit our new arrival.

Cards, flowers and balloons adorned and brightened up the room we were in. Mid-wives and doctors had come and gone and declared everything to be good and we were told we'd be able to take our baby home within a couple of days.

We continued to try and find an appropriate name, scouring the book and our minds for a perfect fit. We had already agreed that the baby's middle name would be my first name if it were a boy and Meg's first name if it was a girl. The surname, mine, of "Gates" was also agreed way before she was born.

Before we were to take her home, we found a name that suited in terms of meaning and fit. "From the edge of the meadow" was the meaning provided by the book which seemed to be a calm and restful reference and our new daughter was to be named "Kelly".

Kelly Megan Gates.

Chapter Four

Over the next few weeks, after returning home to our new house in Fareham, family regularly attended and friends visited to see the new arrival.

During one of her visits, my mother produced an old sepia-toned and well-aged picture of a baby nestling on its front. Incredibly, the baby in the picture, of me when I was several weeks old, looked the spitting image of Kelly.

We registered Kelly at the Fareham Registrar's office within a couple of weeks of the birth. I was so proud to see her name, Kelly Megan Gates, on the birth certificate.

We began to settle into a routine and Kelly moved onto bottled milk after the first couple of weeks on the breast. I was glad Meg had continued with the breast-feeding. Difficult as it was, I think she was glad to have carried on with it too. The best thing about Kelly being on bottles was that we could share the responsibility of feeding and thus the bonding was further shared too.

I made hours of video and took hundreds of photographs. I edited some of the photographs and video together to Aerosmith's "I Don't Want to Miss a Thing" which summed up everything regarding how I felt about Kelly. That song still moves me tremendously today and I rarely get through hearing it without shedding some tears.

I was a very proud father. I took to the duties of bathing, changing nappies, dressing and feeding very naturally. I hated being away from my little girl, even for just a short time.

I carried her picture with me everywhere I went.

We were looking forward to Kelly's first Christmas. Whilst it wouldn't mean much to her, it meant so much to me. We spent Christmas Day at Meg's parents with her family and Boxing Day was due to be spent at my sister's, Deborah, with her family; Mark, her husband, Tasha, Daniel and Christopher their kids, my parents and my other sister, Kathleen and her husband Tony and their daughter Abby.

And then we had our first row since Kelly was born.

We had left Meg's parents' in two separate cars due to the logistics that hadn't been sorted out since Meg started staying at her parents prior to the birth.

I parked along the street and Meg parked her car even further away and out of sight of my sister's house. Meg's car was full of presents and I was worried it might get broken into and the gifts stolen and asked her to move it closer to the house. She refused, not appreciating my concern and, as a result, we argued and the argument continued when we moved inside my sister's house.

I ended up leaving and going home.

Meg came home a short time after and our row continued. It was resolved after a relatively short time although there was still tension between us regarding the incident. In particular, Meg had been upset that we'd argued in front of my family.

I hate confrontation at the best of times and tend to walk away rather than stand up and "have it out" with whomever I'm upset or frustrated with.

*   *   *

Early in the New Year, when Kelly was about three months old, Meg and I had another really big argument. To be honest, as is the case with many arguments, the details have become lost in the mists of time and I can't really remember what it was we specifically argued about. Clearly, it was quite severe and intense.

Meg made the suggestion to go to her parents for a little while. I said that was fine but she wasn't taking Kelly.

We argued some more ending with Meg pulling Kelly from my arms and leaving with her. I was heartbroken. I cried for the longest time at my little girl being taken from me in such a heartless and unfeeling manner.

It seemed to me at the time that Meg didn't want to discuss and resolve the matter and would rather run away than sort the issues out.

The next thing I remember is Meg arriving at the house and collecting various bits of furniture and baby items to provide for Kelly at her parents' house. It was clear she was moving out and back to her parents.

I pleaded with Meg not to take this action as to do so, I felt, was a big step and one that we might not be able to overcome and reverse. I was feeling extremely hurt and helpless and watched in tears as Meg left with the biggest and most important part of my life.

Over the next few months, I implored Meg to come home. I sent her gifts, took her out for drinks and meals, and thing's seemed to be getting better between us.

I was seeing Kelly every other weekend and overnight during the week, usually on a Wednesday. It was hard work, especially with the travel involved, but the precious time spent with Kelly was worth all the hardship in the world.

When Kelly was around nine months old, I remember being at a complete loss when she was crying and refused to sleep. I was at the end of my tether as to what to do and the lack of experience of parenthood was proving difficult. I remember having a tense, terse, conversation with Meg over the phone and shouting at her in respect of what to do to calm Kelly down.

"Can you hear that?" I shouted to her, holding the phone towards Kelly crying in her bedroom.

Meg wasn't that helpful, citing "Now you know what I've had to go through," as a response to what I was going through and seeming not to care or wish to assist to make life for Kelly a little easier.

I had to hang up. I was at a total loss as to what to do. Kelly wasn't taking the bottle, so wasn't hungry, her nappy was clean and everything seemed to be as well as I could make it. I was holding her, walking around, but nothing seemed to help. I just couldn't work out what was wrong.

I remember holding Kelly in front of me and shaking her ever-so-slightly. Not in a violent way, not at all. I would never hurt my little girl. It was more of a judder through my arms, just in frustration, as I was begging her to stop crying.

Eventually, and after calming myself down, I laid her down on the bed and, sitting beside the bed, ran my finger gently from her forehead down her nose repeatedly, something I'd done in the first few months of her little life. It clearly soothed her as she stopped crying almost immediately and her restlessness ceased. Within a few minutes, she was asleep.

I was relieved though absolutely exhausted. I still feel the guilt of not managing the situation better than I did. When I talked to other parents about this kind of situation, they too said they'd had moments like these and they also felt incredibly guilty about similar things they'd done when their patience had run out. I wasn't alone in experiencing this or the feeling I had felt afterwards. But I still feel guilty nonetheless.

* * *

Over the next six to eight months, Meg and I were spending more and more time with each other. We were going out for drinks and meals together and, one evening when we were at her parents, lying together on the sofa, Meg nestled in my arms, I felt we were getting back on track. I kissed her and asked her to marry me.

She said "No."

I felt foolish and embarrassed. "I thought that's what you wanted?" I said, not really expecting an answer. "I thought you wanted commitment, stability?"

Meg went on to explain that it wouldn't be for the right reasons. Upset, I decided to leave. There really did seem no way of going back or rescuing the situation.

Meg told me I didn't have to leave but I felt I had no choice. To stay was too awkward.

I went home and resigned myself to the fact that we would never be a family again.

Oddly enough, with this resignation, things improved between us even more. Our relationship, on a "friends-only" basis worked well for the next couple of years.

We even laughed and joked when shopping in Sainsbury's when talking about Meg's new boyfriend. I'd asked her whether or not he was as good as me. Meg would only say that he was "different".

Everything was co-ordinated between us in respect of Kelly. Kelly became our focus. And the interaction and commitment to Kelly between us was very successful.

We agreed maintenance payments of £300 per calendar month between us, to be reviewed every year. The maintenance was generally for the support of Kelly from providing clothes and food and paying for sundries and consumables used in the support and care of her. It also included a hefty percentage of the fees for child-minding that were required for when Meg was at work.

When Kelly was around eighteen months old, I took over ownership of the house in full having agreed with Meg that a proportion of the equity be paid to her within a certain time – by the end of the calendar year (2001).

Meg moved into a rented house, sharing with her friend Bonnie. I was somewhat dismayed that Meg never consulted me in advance of the fact that she was to be sharing a house with someone I didn't particularly know that well or even approve of.

I came to dislike Bonnie after she lied about something that had happened between us.

Some work colleagues had gotten hold of my phone and sent a message to various people, one of which was Bonnie, saying "I Love You".

Bonnie phoned me when she received the message and I explained what had happened and that it was just my mates having a laugh. Despite this, Bonnie told Meg that I was "coming on to her." Meg chose to believe her friend rather than the truth. I had no time for Bonnie after that.

The house Meg shared with Bonnie wasn't in the best part of Bracknell, being in an area known as "Great Holland's", but it was something she called her own and it meant Kelly had her own bedroom which was a good thing. Whilst Meg had been at her parent's, she'd had everything of Kelly's in her own room which had its problems, not least of which was privacy.

After some time, Bonnie was spending less and less time at the house and eventually she either moved out or it was decided the co-renting wasn't working out. I was actually relieved. I felt Bonnie was a poor influence on Meg and not a good role model for our daughter. Bonnie had a reputation and I was aware that she was seeing several men at the same time even though she was engaged to one of them.

Meg moved into a much nicer area in the Martin's Heron part of Bracknell. The house was a small two-bedroom property but it was more modern than the house in Great Holland's.

I helped Meg with some money and wrote to the council explaining that money given to Meg had been in lieu of the transfer of the house at Jacaranda Close into my name and had been paid in instalments.

This helped Meg in obtaining rental payments from the local council.

I continued making maintenance payments of £300 per month throughout this time and things settled down into a nice routine.

We exchanged photographs of Kelly and were flexible in swapping weekends when we needed to. I started having Kelly every other weekend and for weeks at a time during the holiday periods. We spent most weekends visiting friends and family.

Kelly was growing up fast. She was a good, well natured little girl who was very well behaved. It was always fun being with her. She had an infectious laugh and was, like myself, nearly always smiling. Contented and well used to the situation that she was in with regards to her parents not being together.

Neither I nor Meg had to discipline Kelly very often. She was sent to the "naughty step" when with me just once.

I remember one weekend when Kelly refused to sleep with the door to her bedroom closed. I repeatedly had to get up and shut the door and tell her to "stay in bed" but over and over she got up and pulled the door open.

Finally, I was to work out that she just wanted the door slightly ajar so light from the hall-way came through. A frustrating hour had passed before I worked this out. Kelly had never had a problem sleeping before and I could only assume the moving of houses and a different environment at the new house had brought about a change in her behaviour.

Over the coming weekends, I was able to reduce the gap in the door until we were able to close the door fully.

We had a fun and very close relationship. The house was always full of laughter and happiness when she was around.

We had a "deal" which we confirmed almost every weekend we were together.

"What's our deal, Kelly?" I'd ask her.

"No lies and no secrets." She would always and proudly reply.

The idea of the "deal" was formed whilst Kelly was at her first years in school. It was suggested that it enabled children to tell things to parents and teachers that they may have been told were "our little secret" by people who wanted to do wrong by that child. It worked. Kelly shared things with me about her life at home and what was going on with her mum and also what was happening between her mother and the men in her life.

I was working from home more and more and whilst I had to travel to Bracknell to collect Kelly for her weekend and overnight stays, something I co-ordinated with attendance at the offices of Oracle in Bracknell for my day job, things were good. The relationship between us all worked quite nicely and things were quite settled until Meg got made redundant.

Chapter Five

Once Meg became redundant, everything changed. And it didn't change for the better for either of us.

As Meg wasn't working and was now claiming benefits, I disputed the maintenance in respect of the child-minding costs. Surely, as Meg wasn't working, the requirement for the child-minder wasn't there? Meg argued against this saying she still had to have Kelly at the child-minders as she had "things to do" during the day.

We were unable to come to an agreement and the maintenance ended up staying at £340 per month, an increase which had been agreed earlier in the year on the original sum of £300.

I then received contact from the Child Support Agency. The dreaded CSA[1].

The CSA was created in the late nineteen-eighties, under the government led by Margaret Thatcher. The CSA's main remit was to make non-resident parents responsible for the financial well-being of their children.

With the Child Support Act being passed in 1991, the CSA was empowered. They developed extremely complex systems and formulas to enable them to make non-resident

---

[1] See Appendix One for full history of the CSA.

parents pay to support their children via child maintenance payments.

The CSA and their unfairness, bias towards the parent-with-care (in most cases, the mother) and extreme incompetence are well documented in the press and online.

It's well known that several men named as the Non-Resident Parent (NRP) have committed suicide as a result of the CSA's involvement in their lives and whilst the agency stringently deny that their actions were a contributing factor to those taking their own lives, the evidence – in particular suicide letters that directly blame the CSA and the pressure they bring to bear on the poor souls they affect and their unrelenting pursuit of people with little ability to pay, not to mention two or more systems in operation in parallel which make the entire thing even more unfair, is clear.

* * *

On July 5th, 2001, I became 35 years old. Life was pretty good for me. Despite my commitments to Kelly, I had a lot of free time and invariably spent it with my friends in Portsmouth.

On my birthday, I went for a drink with Dean and another school friend, John. John was a laugh and enjoyed having a drink. During the course of our drinking and celebrating my advancing years we discussed the idea of getting away for a holiday.

We wanted somewhere that was lively, cheap and where we could almost definitely get laid.

"Ibiza." John suggested.

"Superb". I replied.

Within a day or two, the week-long trip was booked for a couple of weeks later. We flew to Ibiza and enjoyed the sun, sea, clubs and copious amounts of alcohol. Neither of us got laid.

During the holiday, I received a phone call. It was from the CSA.

* * *

I had previously received notification from the CSA that I was being pursued for child maintenance. After speaking with them on the phone prior to my holiday, it was explained to me that they had become involved initially because Meg had been made redundant and it was usual when a someone made a claim for child support that the CSA would get involved. It further transpired that Meg had, within a couple of months of being made redundant, obtained a new job and had requested that a private claim for maintenance be continued via the CSA despite there being no formal requirement for this.

I was aghast. Whilst things weren't brilliant between us, we had a reasonable relationship and seemed to be working together for the benefit of Kelly. I was at a loss as to why she wouldn't want to return to our previous agreement and would want to involve any agency with such notoriety as the CSA. Why would she want to destroy the amenable relationship we had?

Involving the CSA would only cause me to stop being as flexible as I was with payments and help when Meg, or Kelly, needed it.

That said, the CSA directed me to their assessments calculation page. I completed the online assessment and it came out at a little under £300. Less than I was paying now anyway! I tried to explain this to Meg and told her that I thought her involvement of the CSA would only have a detrimental effect on our situation and relationship in respect of Kelly but she was as bloody minded and reticent as ever that the CSA should pursue me. I tried to convince her that she might receive less money than she was already getting if the CSA assessed me according to their website assessment.

"My friends said I would get more money from you if I went through the CSA" Meg told me. It was clear it wasn't about what was in Kelly's interests. It was about the money.

It looked like a holiday would be just the tonic after this.

* * *

The woman on the phone to me whilst I was in Ibiza explained that they'd completed the assessment based on the paperwork I had returned. The magical figure they'd come up with, based on my salary and income at the time, was more than £480! I was stunned! £480!! How the fuck had they come up with a figure more than fifty percent higher than their estimate from the assessment made via their website? I could understand it if it was a bit over, but more than fifty percent? Surely it was a joke?

I said that there was surely some mistake but the woman was unhelpful to say the least and refused to assist further. She simply kept stating "It's what the system has come up with."

I was truly staggered. £480 per month to support just one child! That was nearly a third of my take-home salary. It was unbelievable.

The woman explained that I would receive a breakdown of how the sum was determined by post. I thanked her for ruining my holiday and hung up.

* * *

When I returned from my holiday, I saw the assessment from the CSA. It was confusing to say the least. It seemed to ignore half of the information I had provided to them. In particular, it refused to take into account travel costs to and from work.

I contacted them and they simply said I wasn't allowed to have travel costs, despite my office location being more than sixty miles away from my home. They refused to accept my claim for doing a round trip of more than one-hundred and twenty miles, every week-day, costing me more than £250 per month in petrol.

Their reasoning for refusing my claim was because I had a company car. Despite the fact I had to pay for my own fuel, they refused to re-assess me to include my travel costs stating that I had to appeal. The person at the CSA said they would send me the appropriate paperwork.

After several days the forms arrived and I began the appeal process. The paperwork was ridiculous. Pages and pages to fill in. Just to make a simple appeal against one aspect of their decision.

Forms were completed, sent off and, eventually, a date scheduled for the appeal hearing. It would take more than three months just to get the appeal heard. In the meantime, I was to pay the full amount of maintenance. I was barely keeping my head above water paying the £340 per month privately so I didn't know how I was going to manage £480 per month. I supplemented my income with credit card spending.

I attended the offices in Southampton where the appeal was to take place. Meg was also present though I didn't know why she had to be. I refused to speak to her there, still angry at her pursuing a private claim through the CSA when we could have come to an arrangement that suited everyone without involving an outside party. Whatever relationship we had before was already in a downward spiral.

After about half-an-hour of waiting, we were invited into the hearing. Three people, two women and a man, sat behind a long desk. The woman in the middle was reading through my appeal claim and advised me that I had completed the wrong paperwork.

"That was the paperwork I was sent from your office." I explained.

"Well, it's the wrong paperwork." She replied abruptly.

"Why is it only now, when I've come all the way to Southampton some three months since I returned the paperwork for my appeal, that this has come to light?" I asked.

"I don't know." The woman replied.

I was extremely angry. "I suppose if I get the correct paperwork, it'll be another three months until my appeal is heard?" I questioned. "I mean, how do I know if any new paperwork comes as to whether or not it's the correct one?"

The people behind the table shifted uncomfortably in their seats as I began raging.

"I can't believe this!" I said, my voice raised but controlled. "What a waste of time. And just because some incompetent didn't send me the correct forms! I can't believe I was made to come here and that no-one noticed the forms were wrong before this!"

The woman in the middle spoke again.

"I will ensure you are sent the right forms." She said. "We'll get them sent to you right away."

I was livid. Not only had I wasted time and petrol getting to the hearing, I was also going to have to go through the whole process again! This, as I was to learn, was simply the first experience of several I was to have in relation to the incompetence of the CSA.

Chapter Six

The next day, having calmed down, I phoned Meg. I explained to her that having to re-appeal the petrol costs and wait another three months would put me in dire straits financially especially if I had to continue paying £480 per month in maintenance.

"I mean £480 for just one child? Surely you don't think it costs that much to support a kid?" I said to Meg.

Meg even agreed with me that this sum was ridiculous. "No, but you wanted to pay £175 when I was out of work."

"That was only because you shouldn't have needed the child-minder and therefore why should I pay that share?" I countered. "It doesn't matter now anyway, because you're back in work and the child-minder's needed." I said.

I decided to offer to return to the payments I was making previously.

"Look, I can barely afford the £340, but I can just about cover it. Can we go back to that and forget about this crap with the CSA? You've got to admit that since they've been involved there's been nothing but grief. Surely you, just like me, want an easy life?" I offered.

"Four-hundred." Meg said.

"I can't do that. I can barely afford the £340. I could maybe round it up to £350, but that's as high as I can go." I told her.

"It's four-hundred or back to the CSA." She said coldly.

I could see I wasn't going to get anywhere and that £400 was better than £480 and with the CSA out of the picture, things might return to some kind of normality.

"I will have to see if my parents can help with the extra fifty-quid," I told her. "Let me call them and ask. I'll come back to you later."

I ended the conversation there and decided to phone back the next day. It was a joke. With four-hundred quid on top of all the benefits she was getting, as well as her salary, she was raking it in. This wasn't in Kelly's interests. As usual, it was about the money and what she could get. But what was my choice? I didn't really have any.

The next day I phoned her back and said that my parents had agreed to cover the extra fifty pounds per month. I told Meg I would set up the standing order so the money transferred directly from my account on the first of each month. I asked Meg to inform the CSA that we had a private arrangement and that I was paying her £400 per month in lieu of child maintenance payments.

I also wrote to the CSA informing them of this to cover myself in the eventuality that Meg didn't notify them of the change in circumstance. Last thing I wanted was the CSA taking money from my account when I'd already paid Meg. Given their processes, any such error would be severely time-delayed in respect of a refund, if a refund was ever forthcoming.

My parents were never involved or even consulted in the provision of the extra fifty quid. But I wasn't going to let Meg know that. I never once wanted not to contribute to the welfare of my child. All I wanted was that the payment was reasonable and affordable without putting me into extra debt and that it was realistic in terms of covering Kelly's actual support costs.

Not only that, but I felt that this child was both of ours and that the liability of support for her should be shared. If my half of Kelly's support was considered by the CSA to be £480, then Meg's half should also be £480 by my reckoning. That makes a total of £960 per month, for the support of one child.

However, the CSA doesn't take that view. No matter how much the mother earns, no matter how well off the mother is in terms of circumstance and money, none of this is taken into account in the CSA's assessment. They simply pursue those who are trying to do the right thing in paying something and ignore those who pay nothing. I heard of several people that were errant, irresponsible and absent fathers who were earning two or three times that which I did. When the CSA caught up with them, their payments somehow came to a tenth or even less than mine did. How was that fair?

Also, because of two different systems in place with the CSA, CS1 and CS2 (which I dubbed Crap System 1 and Crap System 2), you could find yourself paying more than double that which someone assessed on a later date and under the CS2 system was. You were put on one or the other based purely on the date you were initially assessed.

For example, if I were assessed under CS1, which I was, I was liable to pay, for one child, the sum of £480 per month. This equated to more than twenty-nine percent of my take home salary. Under CS2, the sum is capped at fifteen percent. Just above half of what I had to pay. I tried to get moved to the new system but the CSA were having none of it. They insisted the only way this was possible would be if Meg closed the current assessment or claim and a whole new one was re-opened.

With this in mind, and our new private arrangement set up and working reasonably well, I asked Meg to close the CSA assessment down. She refused. She said that she'd been advised, by the CSA, not to close the assessment down. That if she did and I stopped paying, then she'd have to go through a whole new assessment. I explained to her that they'd have to go through a new assessment anyway even if she didn't, but she still refused to disengage the CSA from our situation.

I heard tales of people at the CSA who delighted in giving their clients information like this because they knew it would penalise the father harder. The tales I heard also detailed members of the CSA staff running internal competitions to see who could get the biggest assessment each day out of the many fathers that they were assessing.

Not exactly the most professional and unbiased bunch, eh?

I also tried to appeal against the fact that I was on a different system but was simply told that the only way to get moved from one system to another was to write to my MP. I did, of course, but it turns out the only reason the CSA referred me to my MP was because the MP's were responsible for bringing the legislation in respect of the CSA into being and it was only they who could reverse it.

In fact, I was totally misled by the CSA when they told me to contact my MP because the MP I contacted had no power whatsoever to get me moved from one system to another.

So, not only were they incompetent and unprofessional, they were also liars or people that simply have no understanding of the processes that should be followed.

Chapter Seven

Over the next few months, things settled down into a familiar routine. Kelly was almost three years old and I would again see her every other weekend and for extended time during the holidays.

I continued paying the £400 per month but never contributed, as I had done before, to any additional sundries or urgent needs for Kelly. When Kelly needed new clothes or shoes, it was Meg that bought them from the money I had already provided. Previously, I had been more than happy to supply Kelly with additional clothes and shoes and other bits and pieces as and when she needed them.

As a result, whenever I bought anything with my own money for Kelly, I made sure those items remained at my house. I felt it was a sorry state of affairs.

On a couple of occasions I accidentally forgot one of the items that Meg had supplied for the weekend.

Meg started giving me lists of clothes and items that Kelly had with her when I collected her from the child-minders and stated that "every item must be returned" on the note.

It's not like Kelly didn't have plenty of clothes. She did. My sister donated lots of clothes that my niece Abby had grown out of. So there were plenty.

In the end, I just left the clothes Meg supplied in the bag in the car and clothed Kelly with those I'd bought myself or that my sister had given me.

It was all so petty and needless. But this was to continue and, if anything, get worse.

Kelly was playing at my house one weekend, setting up a little farmyard with some toy animals and sheds and walls and making pens and such using the gates and fences. I thought it was a good time to put some education into her play. As she picked up and assembled the gates into one of the pens, I said "What's that you're making there?"

Kelly told me, "It's a place for the animals to play in."

"And what's that at the entrance?" I asked her.

"Gates" She said.

"And what's your last name?" I continued.

"Griffin." Kelly said immediately.

"What?" I said, surprised that she was thinking her surname was the same as her mother's when she had been registered as "Gates" on the birth certificate.

"Griffin." She repeated. I was aghast and struggled to understand what was going on.

"No, darling, your name is Gates. Kelly Megan Gates." I told her.

"Yes, it used to be that but now it's Griffin." She told me. I couldn't believe what I was hearing.

It turned out that Meg had changed Kelly's surname by deed poll via a cheap service offered for a small sum via the internet. I was shocked. At no time before doing so had she consulted me or even asked me my opinion on the change.

Why had she done this I wondered?

A million thoughts ran through my head. What reason could she have for changing the name? Was it something practical I wasn't aware of or was it because Kelly wasn't mine? I couldn't even believe I'd thought for that instant that Kelly might not be mine.

I decided to consult a solicitor and find out what my position was. I had few rights in respect of Kelly, even though I was her father and named on the birth certificate as such. At that time, un-married fathers didn't have the same rights as married fathers. Since then, this situation has been remedied and the government set in place that all fathers have the same rights whether they've been married to the mother or not.

Because of the situation at the time, Meg could pretty much do what she wished. Meg had already threatened me with not seeing Kelly if I didn't pay the maintenance.

I was recommended to take Meg to court to obtain a Parental Responsibility Order. This order would give me the same rights regarding Kelly as a father who had been married to the mother when the child was born. It was a fairly simple order and my solicitor advised me to get a contact order drawn up at the same time so that Meg's threats of denying me to see Kelly wouldn't hold any water. My solicitor also suggested the name change reversal be included in the court proceedings as there had been no reasonable reason to change the name from Gates, which Kelly had had all her life, to Griffin.

We went to court and I won all three counts. I obtained Parental Responsibility which meant that I could directly contact Kelly's doctor, dentist and her school in future, to request information about her and her well-being. It also gave me rights to have a say in her upbringing, religion, schooling and pretty much any other aspect of her life whilst she was a child.

A contact order was also agreed to my terms despite Meg trying to insist I return Kelly on a Sunday evening. Meg tried to justify this by saying that Kelly was exhausted on her return to school every other Monday morning. I had obtained, from the school, a statement that detailed there was no discernable tiredness or lack of attention when she returned after spending the weekend with me. Not to mention that it was only once every two weeks that Kelly had to get up just a couple of hours earlier.

Meg went on to suggest that Kelly had been late to school on numerous occasions, when in fact I had evidence from the school detailing she'd only been late three times and two of those were when she was in Meg's care.

The judge said that the routine of returning Kelly on a Monday morning, as part of my journey to work, extended the time I had with Kelly. He said this was in Kelly's interests and decreed that the contact remained as it was.

Meg was also ordered to change the name from Griffin back to Gates. Meg had argued that she had "suffered embarrassment" as a result of the name difference when registering Kelly at the doctors, dentists and nursery school. The judge dismissed this ridiculous claim stating that "it was not unusual these days for children to have a different name to that of the mother." In fact, it was in line with tradition and even if Meg had got married then her name would be different again if she were to assume the name of her husband.

Meg was distraught. She was crying uncontrollably when the judge made his decisions. I felt no joy in seeing her upset at all. The judge noted to me that I should not interpret the events of the day as a victory. I was simply glad that the right thing had been done.

As is the ruling with most cases of family law, the claim for costs I incurred in bringing Meg to court were dismissed, even though I won every aspect of my case. I felt this somewhat unfair but there was nothing I could do.

I suspect that the reasoning for it is that to issue costs against the mother could induce unreasonable hardship on the mother and therefore not be in the best interests of the child.

One of the main remits of the courts is the best interests of the children and something I cannot disagree with.

That said, I raise the question as to the undue hardship the father who is forced to court to see justice done because a mother has, at a whim, taken action or refused co-operation with an order or other unlawful or unreasonable act suffers? The maintenance still needs to be paid, even if the father is out of pocket to the sum of more than £4,000 in court costs and solicitor fees.

* * *

On the way home from the court, I phoned my parents and told them of the news. I explained I was just glad it was all over and just wanted to get on with my life and hoped that things between Meg and myself could improve though in reality I doubted they would.

About half-way home, I suddenly started to shudder uncontrollably. My eyes welled up and my throat became dry. And, again suddenly, a huge wave of relief came over me. I felt as if a huge weight had been lifted from me. The build-up and stress of the events of going to court had been immense and I'd had no release from it at all.

It was only half-way home, when I was alone in the car that the relief of what had happened in my favour really came to me.

I wept uncontrollably. I was shaking and breathing very heavily. I cried so much that I could barely see out of the windscreen and as a result nearly crashed the car!

Chapter Eight

Once the court case was over, things seemed to get better for a time between Meg and me.

Whilst not brilliant, things were at least civil and over the next couple of years the routine of having Kelly every other weekend and during the holidays seemed to work quite well.

I made my own arrangements with my family when I had Kelly and had another engagement or work commitment. Trying to get Meg to swap weekends or be reasonable regarding dropping Kelly back early, was like getting blood from a stone.

Meg did everything in her power, which was all she had left now that I had Parental Responsibility and a contact order in place, to make life as difficult as possible when I needed assistance with moving a weekend or some other arrangement to get Kelly back in time for school. It just wasn't worth the hassle and I managed to liaise with my parents and Kathleen, my youngest sister, when I needed cover.

All was pretty good. Or so I thought.

* * *

Kelly started school, Reception, at New Scotland Hill School in Little Sandhurst, in 2003. Surprisingly, Meg had actually involved me in the decision-making process regarding the school she'd chosen whereby I was informed of the prospective school and made arrangements to visit and see the environment our daughter would be growing up in.

It was a really nice school in a nice area and the teachers were friendly and there were outdoor areas including creative zones and quiet areas which the children could utilise depending on their requirements day to day.

Kelly looked so smart in her new uniform and I arranged with Meg to join her and Kelly to take her to her first day at school.

We took photos outside the main gate and I was very proud that she looked so good. Kelly loved to read books and I knew she'd do well. She got on well with other children and whilst there was the usual leadership struggles, albeit minor, when she played with friends, there were never any issues with her blending in socially.

As Christmas approached, I realised that there was probably a school play that Kelly would be involved in. Unfortunately, I found out too late and the event had passed. I also found out that Meg, Meg's mother Barbara, and two other members of Meg's family had attended. I was surprised I'd not heard any mention of it. I asked Meg why she'd not involved me in this or included me in the invite. Her response was unreal:

"I'm not going to lay it on a plate for you, David," She said. It's up to you to contact the school and make your own arrangements."

I was upset by this. I had missed Kelly's first school play. Meg had seen fit to take the two tickets that the school later told me were intended for me and had passed them on to her own family.

I had to tell Kelly, who was also very upset that I'd not been to see her in her first school play, that I was sorry and explain to her that "Mummy never told me about it." I told Kelly it was partly my fault because I should have realised, but sometimes these things get missed. I couldn't hide my upset from her at her mother's seemingly deliberate actions to prevent me from attending. I promised her I would never miss another one of her school plays again.

I attended the parent's evenings whenever possible, making my own private arrangements with the school to see Kelly's progress. I also contacted the school and asked them to send me the same materials and newsletters that Meg would have access to that Kelly would normally bring home with her after school. This would prove to be a sporadic occurrence and several times I had to chase up the school to obtain the same newsletters and information that Meg was privy to. It was a similar story with the dentists. I had to contact them to find out what work, if any, had been done.

In the end, I started checking the school website on a regular basis to keep myself up-to-date. I never missed another event and was pleased to see Kelly at her first Sports Day, where she did very well coming 1st, 2nd and 3rd in several events, and in the subsequent Christmas Plays. I made sure to attend the plays on the alternative day to which I knew Meg was in attendance to avoid any kind of conflict. The last thing I wanted was to repeat the events of the first play I attended where there was glaring and whispering from Meg and her boyfriend, Joe.

I personally had no problem with Joe. He seemed a reasonable guy and Kelly liked him and maybe it was his influence with Meg that resulted in the calm that occurred during the time she was with him. He had a good job, fitting LCD televisions and whilst we were only in each other's company a few times, it was civil and good natured, even talking about football on one occasion.

Meg surprised me then, some weeks after, by telling me Joe didn't want me coming to the flat to collect Kelly. I was confused. Had I done something untoward? Had I offended him in some way? I didn't have a problem with him so why did he have an issue with me? It was bizarre but collecting Kelly from the flat was something that would, on occasion, be inevitable so the request for me not to attend was somewhat ridiculous.

Also, collecting Kelly from school or from Meg's parents brought some interesting problems of its own. On one occasion, Kelly's cardigan and coat were very dirty. Considering, at this time, I was only being allowed to have a bare minimum of clothes for the weekends I was having Kelly, having clean clothes was a priority as I wouldn't ordinarily have time to wash and dry them before she was due to wear them over the weekend. In time, this became less of a problem as I built up a supply of clothes handed down to me from my sister whose daughter had grown out of them, her being a couple of years older. But some of the email exchanges were fraught, at the least:

From me (following collecting Kelly at the end of a half-term holiday week):

Kelly's cardigan (and coat) was absolutely filthy. I managed to wash her cardigan last night, fortunately I realised with enough time to get it sorted, but was surprised how dirty it was considering she hadn't been at school for a week and you had plenty of opportunity to wash it in that time.

Her shoes could do with a polish once in a while. Even this morning, before the new term had started, they were all scuffed and worn; something a little bit of polish can improve the look of immensely.

There had also been an issue regarding Kelly's attendance of dance classes. Meg wanted Kelly to attend a dance school in Bracknell on Saturday mornings. If I had agreed to this, I would have been collecting Kelly from Bracknell on Friday evening, driving to Fareham, and then returning to Bracknell on the Saturday again on the weekends that she was with me. Then back to Fareham and then back up – a round trip of one-hundred and thirty miles in total! Miles that I had to pay petrol for!

I managed to find a really good dance school, called Stagecoach, in Winchester, which was equidistant from both of us. I informed Meg of my find and was even willing to pay for the classes myself but Meg flatly refused.

When I had Kelly following the inability for a compromise regarding the dance classes, Kelly mentioned that her mother had told her that I refused to let Kelly go. This was not the case and as I refused to lie to Kelly I told her exactly what had happened. I followed up with an email to her mother after Kelly was taken to school on the Monday:

Kelly also commented over the weekend that the reason she wasn't able to go to dance classes was because you had told her "Daddy said no". As you know, this is absolutely not the case as I was more than willing to compromise on the location of said classes but you were unwilling to do so despite my best efforts. I would therefore appreciate it if you would refrain from placing the blame on such events on me, and instead better explain to our daughter the reasons why she is not able to take part in such activities.

Meg's response to the above emails was typical:
You really need to grow up and stop sending such ridiculas [sic] emails. You [sic] pettiness always seems to surprise me!

I did infact [sic] polish Kellys [sic] school shoes before you returned her clothes and with the current weather are you surprised her rain coat gets dirty.... Kelly knows why she is unable to attend a dance class at the moment and that is because you would not allow her to attend a class close to home.

I really wish you would stop all this and get on with your own life and leave me to mine!

Kelly may have had a week off but I didn't...I still had to work and sort Kelly out every day.....something you found difficult when I went on holiday...working and getting her to school / child-minder every day!!!

Like I have said previously and I will say again....unless you have something constructive to say I would rather you not say anything at all!!

I eventually enrolled Kelly into a dance class, near to where I was living with my girlfriend, Lois, every other weekend. She enjoyed the time and socialising opportunity that it gave her but not being there every week meant that she probably felt excluded compared to the other children in the class that were present at most week's rehearsal's and lessons. That said, the dance class tutor said Kelly performed very well and picked things up quickly. With a more regular attendance structure, there was no doubt she would have been able to excel at dancing.

Chapter Nine

In February of 2005, I was made redundant by Oracle. I'd been with the company for nearly fourteen years and knew I would get a good pay-out. Over the last year with Oracle, whilst I worked as a Critical Account Manager, the platform that I was responsible for handling account issues of became more and more stable. As a result, the number of accounts becoming critical grew less and less. It simply became a matter of time until Oracle took an opportunity to make me redundant.

When Oracle took over PeopleSoft, I could have applied for another role within the company, but having been there for so long I felt it was as good a time as any to take stock, re-evaluate my life and career, and move on.

I received a year's salary, tax free, and I took the chance of starting up a motorcycle luggage retail business. Importing goods that I'd seen whilst in Australia the year before, from a company called Strapping Stuff. I invested more than half of my redundancy into starting up the business and stocking up with goods.

Within five months, I started trading and sales grew slowly via the press product reviews, word-of-mouth and the motorcycle shows I attended, demonstrated and sold at. Unfortunately, the products needed extensive advertising and bulk importing in order to make it truly successful – all of which cost money I no longer had - and it remained a small internet retail outlet. Whilst it was successful, it struggled to make enough of a profit that would enable me to earn a living from it.

As I was unemployed, the CSA instructed me that I was not obliged to make any maintenance payments to Meg. My redundancy money couldn't be touched by them either as it wasn't considered to be an income. I was able to sign on to the dole after my garden leave expired three months after my redundancy was formalised.

As I was effectively still living off the money I had from my redundancy, I offered Meg the dole money as a goodwill gesture to help with Kelly's welfare. I asked her to refrain from involving the CSA in this arrangement as I didn't know what effect that it could have on my dole money and I also knew that with any CSA involvement there were invariably complications or problems. This would come to be somewhat of an understatement.

Meg flatly refused and said that the CSA would be made aware of any monies that I paid her. I couldn't understand her reasoning. Here I was, offering her my entire dole money, some £240 per month, and she wasn't willing to exclude the CSA from it. I couldn't believe she would again cut her nose off to spite her face with such a refusal of help. Was I being unreasonable? I didn't think so. I told her that if she was going to involve the CSA, then she could forget it. Even now I still think her decision was mad. Who the hell turns down free money?

Over the next few months, I would also receive numerous phone calls and faxes from the CSA and the Department of Work and Pensions at the Strapping Stuff office number. They were asking for confirmation of "David Gates" working for Strapping Stuff along with salary details, hours worked etc.

I phoned them back and told them each time that I didn't work for Strapping Stuff. Technically, this was true. I didn't "work" for Strapping Stuff. I *was* Strapping Stuff. It was my business. I explained that there were no wages paid to David Gates in my communications with them also, as at that time I wasn't drawing anything for myself from the business as I had to pay for the imports from whatever money came in from sales.

Despite this, within a few months of me signing on, I was summonsed into the Job Centre for an interview, under caution, regarding my role and income from Strapping Stuff and all monies attached to that which suggested that I should not have been receiving the Jobseeker's allowance that I had been. It seemed that someone had reported me for benefit fraud and had suggested to the social security and benefits office that I was working for and receiving wages from Strapping Stuff.

I was interviewed in very intimidating circumstances and whilst I was confident I'd knowingly done nothing wrong, having to deal with these people whose suspicious-minded nature is to suspect and convict you of the fraud you're accused of was still a worry.

I was allowed to bring a representative and was able to find a solicitor who would be engaged at no cost to me. I wasn't informed of the fact I could get a solicitor for free – I managed to find that out, almost by accident. By coincidence, talking to a solicitor to see how much it would cost to have them with me during the interview, I was informed of a specific type of service some solicitors undertake that help people who need representation in these circumstances. The solicitor charges the DWP (Department of Work and Pensions) for their services for the initial interviews. Typically, the DWP refused to suggest the information that this service was available to me. The paperwork simply says you can have a solicitor represent you but it gives no direction that the costs of doing can be covered by the DWP. I'm not saying they went out of their way to not provide this information, but the lack of knowledge of the staff of the DWP and the paperwork in respect of this specifically falls a long way short in indicating this.

At the interview, I produced all of my books for the business, all of my paperwork regarding my redundancy as well as bank statements and passport and other proofs of identification. I also gave them access to and produced details of all of my PayPal expenditures and incomes.

The whole interview was formally recorded on tape, just as if it would have been if I was in a police station being interviewed in relation to a crime.

I gave details of every piece of work that I'd done that I'd been paid for, something which I'd informed them of and which had proved to be a bureaucratic nightmare when doing so whenever I signed on.

We went through every single document I supplied, every transaction on every bank statement, every piece of money I'd spent or received since I was made redundant. It was a nightmare.

Eventually, I realised that the DWP officers had missed the fact that a significantly high salary which I received had actually equated to being part of my redundancy payments. Despite them having the paperwork with this detail on it, right in front of them, they had missed it entirely! As a result, it appeared that I had more money than I was claiming to have had at the time – which may have affected whether or not I could have received the Jobseeker's Allowance payments.

It was finally sorted out when they realised their huge error but it gave me little consolation in vindicating that I'd been honest and open with them from the start.

Even my solicitor made comment to me that the whole thing had been farcical as a result of their mistake.

It was clear however that someone was trying to cause me difficulties and get me into trouble and I was going to have to be even more vigilant than I ever had been in order to ensure that my situation wasn't made any worse.

Despite not having any evidence to conclusively prove it, I always felt that the DWP had been tipped off by Meg. The timing was the main key to this as it followed an error on my part whereby I inadvertently emailed Meg from my Strapping Stuff account. Having done so, she would have been able to see the domain name and simply looked up the website which had details corresponding to my home address. It seemed too much of a coincidence that shortly after having made this mistake, I started receiving the faxes, phone calls and was called to the final interview under caution.

Some say I was being overly paranoid. I'm really not so sure in this instance.

Chapter Ten

It was whilst I was unemployed that I met Lois via an online dating agency.

We had chatted online having exchanged messenger ID's and seemed to get on well and arranged to meet to see how we'd do face-to-face.

Lois lived in Poole though said she was happy to come to Fareham and we decided to meet in the car park of TGI's Friday's, just off Junction 9 of the M27.

At around 1.00 PM on the day we'd decided to meet, Lois phoned me and said, "I'm here."

"What?" I said, confused.

"I'm here, in TGI's car park." She confirmed. I had been expecting us to meet in the evening.

"Fuck!" I said. "Fuck. Fuck. Fuck. Fuck. Fuck!"

Lois laughed.

"Give me ten minutes." I said. "You'll have to take me as I am as I've not even shaved. Wasn't expecting you until tonight!"

"Okay," Lois said, "See you soon."

I ran around the house, hastily spraying bathroom cleaner and bleaching the loo, making the bed and pushing clothes that were previously on the floor of the bedroom into the laundry basket. Not that I was expecting her to see the bedroom of course, but if she should need the toilet she'd pass by and I didn't want her to see me as an untidy person. Generally speaking, my house – with the exception of my office – is usually kept neat and tidy.

I had a quick wash, put a shirt on hastily, splashed some after-shave on and sprayed almost a whole can of deodorant across my person.

I dashed from my house to TGI's as quickly as I could and found Lois sitting in the doorway of her car, her shoes kicked off airing her feet, waiting for me at the far side of the car park.

I apologised for my appearance and we said polite hello's and decided to have a drink in TGI's. I was glad of this as it would allow me some time to relax. Lois put her shoes back on, locked her car and we went to the TGI's bar.

Lois was blonde and beautiful and looked quite different from the picture I'd seen of her previously. The picture showed her as looking quite stern and with slightly shorter hair but the person in front of me was gorgeous, friendly and smiling.

She nipped to the loo at one point and I texted my mate Dean:

"I'm sitting here in TGI's next to a gorgeous blonde! Can't believe it!" I told him.

Lois returned and I decided to give her an option to opt-out of going any further. I didn't want her to feel obliged to stay if she didn't want to.

"I don't know what you would like to do," I said, "But we can either have another drink here or go on somewhere else, or if you want to get off then that's fine too." I suggested.

"No, that's okay. We can go on somewhere else. That would be nice." She said.

I was beyond chuffed. She actually wanted to spend more time with me!

Lois offered to drive as she wasn't drinking anyway and we drove from TGI's down to Old Portsmouth, with me showing highlights and landmarks along the way. She drove fast in her Honda Accord which half-scared and half-excited me.

We talked about a variety of things and after we'd parked up and were walking towards the pub called The Still and West, I jauntily touched her shoulder with my fingers and said, shrilly, "We haven't even talked about sex yet!"

This made her laugh and we enjoyed another drink at the pub before Lois drove us back to my house. I was to later find out that my silliness in respect of us having not talked about sex on our first date was to be the endearing factor for Lois.

I think the effect of alcohol allowed me to be much more relaxed and the earlier than expected meeting didn't allow me time to get nervous, so I was probably behaving more like my normal self than I would have been in the same situation otherwise.

Once at home, I made a cup of tea for Lois and sat on my large sofa, half-expecting her to sit on the two-seater to one side.

She sat next to me, leaning her back against my chest and nestled into the crook of my arm, pulling my arm around her saying, "You can relax now."

It felt really natural and we sat and chilled and listened to music and chatted. All too soon, Lois had to leave to travel back to Poole. I walked her to the door.

We said our goodbyes and Lois kissed me and then danced to her car. I was on cloud nine.

It was to be the start of a beautiful relationship. One which very nearly ended almost as soon as it started. After just two weeks, Lois broke up with me.

The excuse she gave at the time was around wanting me all to herself. She said that having to share me with Kelly was something she didn't want to have to do. It was made all the more ridiculous in the week that followed us breaking up that she was never online so it was impossible to talk to her.

I was holding back on texting but inside I was beside myself. After a week, I relented. I texted her.

"I promised myself I wouldn't do this," I told her, "But I just can't stand the thought of never seeing you again. It's killing me."

She texted back saying that she was feeling the same way and it was totally mad. Lois would eventually, two months after we'd met, tell me the real reason for breaking up with me:

"The only reason why I broke it off with you was because I was falling for you. I didn't want to fall again and get kicked in the nuts like last time." She told me via instant messenger. "That time I was without you was horrible."

Lois went on to tell me she loved me. I told her I loved her too. "You are the only man who's ever made me feel complete." She told me. "You are the calm in my storm, you are the only one who has made me feel everything will be alright."

We spoke about how scared we both were and joked about how committed we were to each other. Lois would quote from the television show, A League of Gentleman: "You're my wife now Dave." which always made me laugh.

We talked about my relationship with Kelly, how often I saw her and that there was no way I could not make Kelly the priority in my life.

Over the next few months we spent time together at both the flat she rented above her parents' house in Poole, and at mine.

I got on well with her parents and Lois joked about how impressed her Dad was with my knowledge of computers and in helping him resolve issues on those he owned. She first indicated that from her Dad's perspective, "the sun shines out of your arse!"

On a subsequent visit where I fixed an issue with his anti-virus, she texted me to tell me "the sunlight has been replaced by a nuclear fusion glow."

Lois was funny, sexy and sassy. She was five years younger than me but we got on famously. I'd never been out with a girl before that I never argued with. In the first two years we were together, we didn't argue once.

*   *   *

I'd been cautious about introducing Kelly to Lois and vice-versa because, for such a long time, Kelly had never seen me with anyone and because of the things Lois had previously said about Kelly being in my life.

I told Kelly I had a girlfriend and asked her if she would like to meet her. Kelly said "Yes." We talked about it several times before I arranged for them to meet each other.

Lois gave me some cushions and an Elmo toy for Kelly which I gave her before she met Kelly. Texts I exchanged with Lois at the time showed what Kelly had thought.
22.12.10 (From me to Lois)
Kelly liked the cushions and she loves Elmo. She took him to bed and said to say Thank you. I will show her W and G

(Wallace and Gromit) stuff tomorrow. She would like to meet you too.

22.16.43 (From me to Lois)
She was really cool about meeting you.

22.27.54 (From Lois)
Crikey, wonder what she'd be like if I got her the furry blanket as well!!!!

22.32.49 (From me to Lois)
She loved how soft they were and the fact they were HER cushions.

I introduced them to each other at the end of October. After Lois had left, to attend a show later that evening, I got Kelly's reaction and communicated it to Lois via text.

18.54.30 (From me to Lois)
Kelly said she likes you and thinks you are very funny. She also said she hopes you have a nice show tonight. Me too. D. Xx

Lois also clearly liked Kelly.

19.16.18 *(From Lois)*
Tell her I like her too!! Just about to see the show. Hope it's good! X

Over the next couple of months, and leading up to Christmas, it was clear Lois accepted Kelly being in my life. She texted to tell me "Missing you both!!" and when we were all due to have Christmas dinner with the rest of her family, including Lois's brother, her sister Tricia and Tricia's partner, she texted telling me she "Wished it was just me and you and Kelly."

I needn't have worried about them meeting. Not only did they get on well but Lois's dog, Brian, would prove to be a nice go-between. Kelly loved him. Lois was as funny and nice with Kelly as she was with me.

I joked that Lois and Kelly loved Brian more than they did me. They never denied it.

Lois and I fell more and more in love and a year after we'd met, on my birthday, with just minutes to go before midnight and the end of my birthday, I asked Lois to stand in front of the sofa. Once she had done so, I slid off the sofa, pulling the ring-box that I'd concealed earlier from its hiding place between the cushions, opening it as I knelt on one knee and asked Lois to marry me.

She screamed. And screamed and screamed.

It was okay. It was a happy, excited scream. She was almost jumping up and down on the spot. I looked nervously at the clock. I wanted her to say yes before midnight so that she'd give me the best birthday present I could ever wish for. I reminded her.

"You haven't given me an answer." I said.

"Yes!" She exclaimed. "Yes, yes, yes!" I stood up and took the ring from the box and put it on her finger. It was one she'd liked and pointed out to me some time previously.

We hugged and kissed. Lois rang her sister, Tricia. Tricia screamed.

Lois ran downstairs and told her parents. They were somewhat calmer as I'd already asked Lois's father for permission to ask her. He was a military man, having spent most of his life in the army, and I figured he'd welcome the traditional way of doing things.

"Do you love her then?" He had asked me.

"Yes. Absolutely." I told him.

I'd found my soul mate. The one I'd been searching for my entire life. I'd never met anyone like her before. She was "the one".

* * *

During the following two years after my redundancy, I was able to have Kelly more extensively during the holidays. Kelly looked forward to spending time with me and we managed a number of firsts which I was very proud to have been involved in during this part of her life.

Kelly learnt to ride a bike, learnt to swim, and had her first foreign holiday which included a flight to Cyprus. My friend Chris was getting married to Rachel and they were holding the wedding there and had invited us along. Despite being at the tail end of my redundancy money I decided to spend what I had left on an experience Lois, Kelly and I would never forget.

Getting a passport for Kelly to be able to take her out of the country was problematic and not without worry.

I broached the subject with Meg well in advance, by about six months. In September of 2005, I explained the requirement was for my friend's wedding the following March and we'd really like Kelly to be able to be there. Kelly was friends with Chris's daughter, Sofie, and had been directly invited as well and it was too good an opportunity to miss. Kelly had already been let down in respect of going to Disneyland Paris, by her mum, the previous year. I told Meg I'd be happy to pay for the passport but it seemed Meg had some concerns about me not returning Kelly to the U.K., which was absurd. I had a home in the U.K., my family was there, and I was running a business from there. There was no way I could leave England. Yet, Meg still had doubts.

I suppose I can understand her worries to some degree but if I was going to take Kelly out of the country and keep her there, would I really have been forewarning Meg of my intentions? It was far more likely, had I wanted to, that I would have collected Kelly of a normal weekend and simply not returned. The passport would not necessarily have been a problem if I had been intent on kidnapping her either.

I sent Meg a cheque for the amount to obtain the passport in the latter part of the year before we were due to travel. Three months passed and the cheque hadn't been cashed and the passport office confirmed that no passport for Kelly had been applied for. What was Meg playing at?

I phoned Meg to ask what was going on. She said that she had *just* applied for the passport and I remember thinking it was just as well that the country we were going to didn't have requirements that you had to have a valid passport for at least a number of months prior to travel. Also, the cheque was never cashed by the passport office. That meant Meg had paid for it herself. None of this made any sense to me or Lois and we just prayed that she had genuinely applied for it and that it was there with her in time for our holiday.

Eventually, Meg confirmed that the passport had arrived. As I liked to be somewhat organized with regards to tickets, insurance, passports and paperwork before I go away, I asked if I could have it in advance of the holiday but Meg insisted we would only get the passport on the day of travel. She was really paranoid about this. I told her that this wasn't good enough or even practical as to travel from Poole to Sandhurst to collect it on the way to the airport, was significantly out of our way and the last thing we needed on the way to an airport was a diversion. Meg finally relented and said she would allow me to collect the passport when I collected Kelly on the Friday prior to our traveling over that weekend.

Meg also insisted that I give her the details of the hotel we were staying at and contact numbers whilst we were there. I was more than happy to do this to allay any fears she had.

Kelly confirmed that the passport had arrived on the following weekend and told me how she'd seen her photo in it, so at least we knew it was there. It did seem that Meg was making the entire process and situation more complicated than it needed to be.

We collected Kelly and the passport and I promised Meg I would look after Kelly during the holiday. Why wouldn't I? I said I'd get Kelly to ring home once we were there, which she did.

During the holiday itself, Meg rang every single day which became rather bothersome. Meg's reaction, via text message, if we weren't able to answer the phone or didn't respond within an hour or so was stressful to say the least. It got to the stage where I had to tell Meg to stop phoning and that everything was fine. Not only was it expensive for me, having to pick up the majority of the cost of the call being abroad, but it was somewhat intrusive. It really was about time Meg started trusting me with our daughter.

The holiday itself was great. Kelly enjoyed the hot weather and loved learning foreign language phrases to say "Hello" and "Thank you" to the locals. Kelly had managed to learn to swim without flotation aids shortly before we came away and she spent most of the time in the pool.

It was also the first holiday Lois and I had shared with Kelly and I was worried about how this would affect my relationship with Lois. Spending the odd weekend with someone else's child was not so bad in the grand scheme of things, especially when most of those weekends weren't spent with Lois anyway. But being with her twenty-four-seven for a whole week was a different matter entirely. I made provision to give Lois time to be on her own, which meant I could spend quality time exploring the town we stayed in, and the beach, with Kelly.

Kelly was also supplied with a disposable camera to capture the holiday and be able to show her mother her experience once she returned home. Lois and I believed that it was an attempt, by Meg, to find out what Lois looked like. We successfully managed, throughout the entire holiday, to keep Lois out of the photos that Kelly took. We took plenty of photos with Lois on my own camera though, so Kelly would be able to have those memories for the future.

Kelly was returned to her mother's on the way back from the airport. I genuinely absent-mindedly forgot to give over the passport and, in the subsequent weeks, Meg would demand its return and even made the suggestion that I was keeping it with suspicious intentions. What on earth was I going to do with a child's passport?

All in all, Meg's behaviour was everything we'd come to expect. Her reticence at applying for and handing over the passport without fuss was ridiculous. Phoning every single day indicated some severe trust and insecurity issues. I hoped that, after Kelly was returned and the positive experience that the holiday had on her, that Meg would start to see I had no ill-intentions towards her maternal role.

There came a time when my redundancy money began to run out and I could no longer live on the paltry allowance that the government gave me. I could never understand how people seem to live on the dole for years and years and seem to be in the pub every night or have a lifestyle that far outweighs that you'd expect from someone on the level of money that the government provides.

I had tried to obtain housing benefit, or some kind of assistance with the mortgage, but the benefits office was unhelpful in every respect.

When I asked for help initially, when the money I had that covered the mortgage payments began to run out, they told me I'd have to wait at least nine months before they could offer any assistance. I tried to explain to them that I needed the help there and then and that if I waited nine months, my house would have been repossessed. They were unrepentant and I had to put the house on the market for fear of having it repossessed and still being liable for any outstanding mortgage. To lose the house was one thing, but to still be liable for the costs associated with it once it's been taken from me was another.

The house sold reasonably quickly and I was able to move into my girlfriend's flat. Lois's flat needed work and I made busy during this time and redecorated the main and spare bedrooms to a standard that made them inhabitable and gave us the spare bedroom for Kelly to use when she stayed with us at weekends.

Losing the house was one of my biggest regrets. I'd worked all my life to get the home of my dreams and it was lost. I'd made some bad choices, some poor consolidation of debts, run up further debts when trying to pay off more debt. Even after I'd sold the house, I still owed a fortune to various credit card and loan companies. Everything had just spiralled out of control.

I also continued to look for a job. It was hard work. I checked the websites every day, the paper every week, and even sent letters to managing directors in an attempt to offer my services. I managed to get occasional work through the company that Lois worked for. It was mostly manual labour and just helping out, but it was a reasonable hourly rate and gave me something to do as opposed to just sitting in front of a computer all day.

The business, Strapping Stuff, was suffering and not bringing in nearly enough money to live on. It was beer money at best. It needed serious investment, which I didn't have, to make it succeed or take off, but there were problems in getting stock quickly and advertising was expensive to say the least. There was no point even trying to get a loan or investment to help the business out as I was too much of a risk given the levels of debt I had at the time.

After a while, and several reincarnations of my Curriculum Vitae, I started getting occasional interviews. I tried to work the interviews around my commitments to Kelly, but on at least one occasion this was not possible. One role I had applied and secured an interview for insisted that I attend early on a Monday morning to meet the manager and go through the process that would hopefully lead me to employment. As the interview was on a Monday following a weekend that I was scheduled to have Kelly, this would mean having to return Kelly early, on the Sunday evening, to allow me to attend. I contacted Meg the moment I found out about it and asked her if it would be possible to drop Kelly off on the Sunday.

The first exchange, via text, was almost a week before I had to return Kelly but the conversation went as follows:

23rd August 2006

12.04.14 (From me)

Forgot to mention that will have to bring Kelly back on Sunday evening this week.

18.34.33 (From Meg)
Sorry im away till late Sunday night.

18.35.17 (From me)

I will have to drop her at your mum's then.

18.39.33 (From Meg)
They r on holiday. If u couldn't have Kelly as agreed u should have said b4 u collected her.

18.41.01 (From Meg)
My mum isn't the answer 2 ur access problems. U cant assume she can do it.

18.43.32 (From me)

You will have to collect her from my mum's at your convenience from Sunday evening onwards.

18.47.57 (From Meg)
I just told u im away! U should have said something before!! U will have 2 sort something else out 2 bring her back on Monday morning.

18.50.49 (From me)

Not possible. You will have to pick her up from my mums Monday. My mums number is xxxxxxxxxxxxx

18.53.33 (From Meg)

I don't want ur mums number. It is your responsibility 2 bring Kelly back on Monday mornings unless otherwise agreed at it wasn't. Sorry but this is your problem not mine.

18.58.20 (From me)

She will stay at my mums until you collect her then.

19.01.25 (From Meg)

Very grown up. I'll just remind the court of the contact agreement u requested. She is 2 b returned as agreed or I will call the courts and the police.

19.09.27 (From me)

Fine. She will be at my mums from Sunday evening.

There was no further exchange for the remainder of the week. I'd given almost a week's notice and Meg was being unhelpful in the extreme in not helping me return Kelly. Lois suggested I call Meg's bluff and on the Sunday I sent Meg the following:

1st September 2006

10.57.03 (From me)
Kelly will be at my mum's from approx. 18.00 this evening. Collect her at your convenience.

11.31.22 (From Meg)
Bring her home.

11.56.00 (From Meg)
Bring her home at 6. Let me know that's ok.

    I must have responded positively, but no longer have the text detail.

11.57.55 (From Meg)
Fine I will leave early. This will not happen again.

    I told Meg that she wasn't being amenable or co-operative. Her excuses, when she stated, quite suddenly, that no-one else – not her parents, her sister nor her brother, or anyone else for that matter were available to help out, mysteriously all "being away" at that precise weekend/day were ridiculous.

In the end, I had to call her bluff. Lois had been right. I told Meg that she would have to travel to my parents to collect our daughter as I would not be available to drive Kelly to school the following morning due to the time of the interview. Eventually Meg relented but her stubbornness knew no bounds. In every respect of changing arrangements, even if they benefitted her, Meg would refuse.

It seemed that Meg frequently liked to cut her nose off to spite her face. I also suspected that Meg's behaviour was as a result of finding out Lois and I had gotten engaged. Maybe she was jealous, I don't know, but her behaviour was getting worse.

The stress even had an effect on my relationship with Lois. But we talked about it and I determined it was best to keep Meg's unreasonable behaviour away from Lois as much as possible. It may have been a portent of what was to come, and I had to check when I felt Lois was being a bit distant from me.

"Are we okay?" I asked her.

"We are ok but I need time to understand why I feel the way I do about Kelly." She told me via text.

Over the next year, we would have several conversations and our first arguments around Kelly's parentage. Lois would repeatedly state her suspicions.

* * *

Just like buses coming along, whereby you wait for one for ages then several come along, I finally got the opportunity for more than one job around late August. The choice was between a start-up communications company where I'd be my own boss and have a share of the business, and a customer-services helpdesk management role. The helpdesk role was about £5,000 per year more and I chased the money.

The other position was likely to be a step in the dark for me and whilst it may have had long-term benefits and a higher return eventually, it was a much bigger risk and didn't give me quite enough to live on month-to-month from the off.

I started in my new role at the beginning of September. Within a few weeks I realised I'd made a mistake. Whilst the job itself was challenging, I was micro-managed by the managing director of the company who was extremely hands-on, except when it came to sacking people. He didn't allow me an opportunity to implement my management skills to the situation they were experiencing which mostly involved high turnover of staff and an inefficient department.

Just as things were escalating within the company to the point where I was going to leave, and as a member of my staff was sacked from my department without my prior knowledge or presence or even opinion on the matter, I was offered another role within another organisation.

I'd been for an assessment day, on a Friday, at Microsoft. On my way home, the person running the assessment day had phoned me.

"We just thought that you would like to know, rather than wait over the weekend to hear, that we've decided to offer you the job." She told me.

I accepted on the spot.

I phoned Lois.

"I got the job!" I told her.

She screamed. I screamed. We both screamed.

Chapter Eleven

I started work at Microsoft in October 2006. The culture and work/life balance that Microsoft provides was similar to that which I experienced when I first started at Oracle some fifteen years previous.

Oracle had become something of a "numbers" company during the time I was there. In the early days of my employment with Oracle, there were summer parties, events, good communication, fairness and respect and recognition for good and hard work. I received a couple of awards during my time there. But, as time went on, and most noticeably following a change in the Managing Director, I frequently felt that the employees were not valued as much as they had been previously.

A lack of respect, people stealing others' work, ego's taking over where common sense should have prevailed, lack of support from management, no recognition – I, and most of the Support organisation in the U.K., received no pay rise during the last six years I was there – all led to a dog-eat-dog culture where only the bottom line mattered. I enjoyed my time immensely whilst there and still have many friends I met during my employment there, but things had changed and the redundancy was timely and welcomed.

Coming to Microsoft was like joining Oracle all over again, but this time the work ethic had lasted twenty years and given the success was not likely to change. I loved it.

Having started employment again, I had to re-enter the world of the CSA and be re-assessed for maintenance. This was complicated by the fact that I was employed in the helpdesk manager role at The Richmond Group for just one month and was evaluated based on my salary there initially. Despite having sent the CSA the salary details from The Richmond Group, someone within the CSA organisation followed-up and re-assessed me almost immediately following my start at Microsoft.

The CSA worked their magic and came up with a figure of £580 per month! For one child this struck me as an outrageous sum of money for maintenance. It no way costs this amount to support a child and no consideration was given for my outstanding debt, outgoings and the fact I was having Kelly every other weekend and during the school holidays and was having to support her and provide her with clothes, furnishings, bedding, food and so on during her time with me.

The CSA, rather predictably, refused to assess me under the new rules scheme that would see that figure halved. I wrote to my MP and the MP responsible for the CSA at the time.

The response was that the CSA processes were being reviewed and "everyone" would be moved to the new system (a third system) from 2012. Given this was 2006, that was six years away! When I asked how long it would take for the reassessment, I was informed all cases would be transferred and reassessed alphabetically. It was anticipated that it would take up to an additional five years following the start in 2012 for all cases to be moved over.

In other words, it could take up to ten years before my case was moved to the new system. By then, Kelly would be almost eighteen and the maintenance would change but not be backdated. There was simply no point in even hoping this new system would sort things out. It was tremendously flawed, most notably in the time it was expected for it to complete.

As before, I had to come to an arrangement with Meg in order to be able to maintain some standard of living. My debts were so extensive that I was barely keeping my head above water, even without the maintenance.

We finally agreed again on a figure of £400.00 per month. I informed the CSA of the arrangement and Meg confirmed it with them also so they would stop harassing me for the maintenance.

I made arrangements with my bank to make the first payment by standing order on the first of the following month, which was about a week following.

On the first weekday of the month, Meg contacted me by text:

2nd October 2006:

13.07.48 (From Meg)
What is going on? Where is the money?! Not a good start is it!

13.28.52 (From me)
Have informed bank. Money should be there in due course.

14.19.07 (From Meg)
And that is likely to be when?

15.07.16 (From Meg)
And that is likely to be when? Hello!

18.18.26 (From Meg)
Don't bother calling tonight we aren't home.

The money went through and was credited to her account on the first working day of the month. Despite this, Meg's impatience and lack of trust that I would keep to the agreement continued. Just one month later, she sent the following text:

1st November 2006

Time unknown. (From Meg)

Ok, I will assume as no money has been received that you are happy for the CSA to continue. This is your daughter you are refusing to contribute for? Some responsible parent!!

Meg frequently referred to me as not being a responsible parent. This went back to the Parental Responsibility order that I had won. Meg's lack of understanding of the meaning of this order continued even after a judge told her she needed to understand exactly what one of those orders were. The courts are very clear and the instructions to the judge in granting the order refer specifically to the statute that says that if the father demonstrates a love and commitment to the child in question, and there are no concerns for the welfare and safety of the child, then the order should be granted.

I paid the maintenance regularly and on time. I looked after Kelly every other weekend and during the school holidays. I supported her and took an interest in everything she did. I took an active interest in her schooling, her well-being, her upbringing. I showed her new things, took her away on holiday, gave her a father that was loving, caring, considerate and committed to her in every respect. In the whole time I was with Kelly, I only lied to her once. Kelly was my world and there's not a thing I wouldn't have done for her despite the pressure and unreasonable behaviour of her mother. An irresponsible parent doesn't do these things.

An irresponsible parent changes the child's name without informing the father. An irresponsible parent forces undue hardship on the father by insisting on a maintenance payment that is far beyond that which it actually costs to support a child and which he can realistically manage to pay. An irresponsible parent cuts their nose off to spite their face in respect of what's best for the child. An irresponsible parent lies not only to the father and the child, but also to themselves. An irresponsible parent denies the father access because of personal reasons unrelated to the child.

It was no wonder then, given the attitude of Kelly's mother, that I took steps to keep our business private. I never disclosed my employer to Meg. It was none of her business and I didn't want her making issues for me with my new job.

She was vindictive enough, given the experience I'd had with the DWP and the Strapping Stuff employment fiasco and I needed to ensure that she knew nothing of where I worked.

This was difficult as I wanted to share where I worked with Kelly. Microsoft have Christmas parties for the kids and I had to take the decision to not have Kelly attend for fear that Meg would find out from Kelly subsequently where the party was held.

There's also a misconception that people at Microsoft are paid extremely well due to the fortune that Bill Gates has amassed as a result of the company's success. This misconception could easily have led to Meg thinking that I was richer than I actually was in terms of salary. With that thought in her head, she would almost have certainly demanded more money. Money I didn't have but which the CSA would take anyway making my life more uncomfortable.

Unfortunately, the CSA's incompetence would lead them to disclose my employer to Meg. One would expect the default to be that such details are not disclosed. Yet, as the non-resident parent (usually the father), you have to directly request that these details be withheld from the parent with care (usually the mother). The default on the mother's side is that none of her details are ever disclosed to the father (or non-resident parent). The CSA say this is to protect the mother and child in cases of domestic abuse. Yet they don't extend this courtesy to the father or non-resident parent.

Further examples of Meg's reliance on the money I was paying was made evident in June 2007:

1st June 2007

08.40.51 (From Meg)
Where is my money from you? We are meant to be going out today!

09.55.49 (From Meg)
can you let me know whats going on! My bank cant see any money coming in and we have been unable to leave for our day trip out.

Given that the maintenance I paid could go into Meg's bank at any time on the first working day of the month, her reliance on funds being available early in the morning and her management of the money that was supporting our daughter, or meant to be, was worrying to say the least. Was she really so poorly-off that she needed my money to fund a day out? Was she really struggling despite the extra £400 a month I was giving her and had been month-to-month for the last nine months before June 2007?

I agreed to part-fund a school-day or event that Kelly attended in June. I agreed to make the payment once I'd been paid and in addition to the maintenance on the 1st July 2007. I transferred the money but inadvertently paid £12.00 instead of £15.00. A difference of just a couple of quid, just a simple clerical error, seemed to make for one hell of an issue:

2nd July 2007

15.40.42 (From Meg)
Can you pay the correct value into my account. I will not chase you again. I agreed to wait till pay day for the money and still you don't get it right. Any future additional payments will need to be made prior to the event.

The aggression was entirely unwarranted. Three quid short and this was the kind of reaction I got. Surely she could have simply said "I received £12.00 instead of £15.00, has there been a mistake?" I could have checked, realised my mistake, apologised and sorted the problem out but Meg had to make it confrontational again.

It also further confirmed that Meg was almost entirely driven by money and the need to make me pay.

Chapter Twelve

During June 2007, Lois and I broke up and I moved back to my parents flat in Havant, near Portsmouth, temporarily.

Lois and I had argued about Kelly and the situation and on-going stress from Meg didn't make it any easier.

Eventually, it had become too much of an issue for us both to contend with and I moved out of Lois's flat. Lois kept suggesting that she couldn't see any of me in Kelly and had doubts as to whether I was her father.

I'd had my own doubts. When Kelly was two years old and the issue of her name-change came apparent, it had prompted me to purchase a DNA testing kit. I'd talked myself out of it and never went through the process of collecting and having the DNA analysed.

It was such a tremendous issue that Lois simply couldn't let go of and I made the decision to move out.

A few weeks later, on my birthday, on the 5th of July 2007, Lois sent me a text.

"Happy Birthday from me and Brian."

I missed Lois immensely. She was everything I'd been looking for, my soul mate, and the only person who truly "got" me. I had never loved anyone as much and had thought we would be together forever. In the first two years of our relationship, we hadn't argued once. It was only the issue of Kelly's parentage that had created a rift between us.

I thanked her for her message and told her I still loved her.

Lois sent me a text back. "I love you but I love you enough to let you go. It fucking hurts but I would rather have this than ten more years of that part of your life."

I left my parents living room and went to my car and phoned Lois. We talked for almost an hour about what we were feeling and why.

I told Lois how important she was to me, how I felt about her, and how I didn't want to lose her. I also understood how she felt and told her I would get a DNA test to finally put this issue to bed.

We agreed that if the result showed I was the father, this would be the end of the matter and we would move on with our lives together.

I made arrangements for a test in readiness for the next time I was due to have Kelly at a weekend. I didn't feel entirely comfortable about it but knew it was the only way to save my relationship with Lois and resolve the nagging doubts I'd had previously.

Lois told me to "come home" and I returned to her flat.

I researched the testing facilities via the internet and found a company called Anglian DNA that specialised in providing tests which they called "relationship tests". The turnaround was fairly quick and within a couple of days I received the kit which consisted of a couple of sealable envelopes and swabs (like long cotton-buds).

My mate Greg urged me not to conduct the test.

"No good can come of it." He warned me.

"It's the only way I can be sure and can put this to bed." I told him.

Whilst Kelly was visiting, over the weekend of the 14th July, I took her to my parents and stayed there with her during that time. Lois felt she couldn't deal with having Kelly at her place at this particular time so I lodged with my parents over the weekend.

I got out the DNA kit and told Kelly I needed to do a test to check her teeth and gums were okay. I hated myself for having to lie to her. I still hate myself for lying to her. It was the first time that I lied to her. It was also the only way to conduct the test without causing her any worry or filling her head with complicated scenarios around parentage. She was just seven and a half and didn't need that kind of worry. It was bad enough for me to have to contend with, let alone place that stress on a seven year old.

As I conducted the test, pushing the swab into her mouth and against her gums and cheeks, I accidentally pressed a little too hard causing Kelly to say "Ouch!" I hugged her and said "Sorry" to her. The last thing I wanted to do was to hurt her in any way.

I placed her swab into the envelope I labelled for her and later took my own sample by swabbing around the teeth and gums in my own mouth in the same way as I had done with Kelly.

I placed both samples into the pre-paid envelope provided and gave myself some time to think about whether or not to send them off.

It was a tough decision. The main part of me was convinced Kelly was mine. We had a connection, similar senses of humour, a Joie-de-vivre that belied anything untoward. I loved her with every ounce of my being, with every inch of my soul. I'd die for her. No question.

Yet, here I was about to possibly undo all of that in order to know the truth. Even when stood in front of the letterbox, I hesitated.

And then it was done. The samples were posted. And now, all we could do was wait.

* * *

Lois and I had been away for most of the weekend when the letter from Anglian DNA came. We arrived home in the late afternoon, on Sunday 29th July, and our mail was piled on the large table that Lois used for private work, in one of the front rooms of her parents' house.

We stood, going through our mail when I came across the letter. I was nervous, anxious, not sure whether or not I wanted to know the contents.

I held it in front of me and Lois instinctively knew what it was. I opened it gingerly and pulled out the contents. A several-page letter was enclosed. The front page of the letter thanked us for choosing the company for the relationship test. The following page had some scientific reference detailing the names of the subjects of the testing and the type of samples along with ethnic origin and identification which was meaningless to me in the context of whether or not I was the father.

The third page of the letter contained the key information as to the DNA results. It read as follows:

Interpretation:

Based on the DNA analysis, the Alleged Father (David Eric Gates) **IS EXCLUDED** as the biological Father of the Child (Kelly Megan Gates).

This result is consistent with the statement that the Alleged Father (David Eric Gates) **IS NOT THE BIOLOGICAL FATHER** of the Child (Kelly Megan Gates).

Our opinion of **NON-PATERNITY** is based on the above noted inconsistencies. The term "inconsistent" means the band sizes of the tested Alleged Father do not match the corresponding paternal band sizes present in the Child.

The document went on to state information around the test itself and a page of "Frequently Asked Questions" stated the meaning behind what "excluded" and "not excluded" meant in the context of the test but by then I'd stopped reading.

I wasn't Kelly's father.

Lois stood, hesitant, waiting for me to give her some indication of what was contained in the letter. I was numb. I could only hand her the document.

Lois read it and exclaimed, "Does this mean what I think it means?" The realisation dawned on her also and she reeled, falling back against the wall a few feet away. Her eyes welled up and I could see she was struggling to hold it together.

She had been right. Her instincts had been bang on, but she didn't react in the way one would expect someone who is proven to be right to react. The only thing I can think of is that she was experiencing the pain which I should have been.

"I need a drink," Was all I could muster. "I'm going to get some drink. I'll be back in a minute."

When I left the house, the flat, I left Lois in the front room, standing beside the giant work table she used to prepare and make curtains and other soft furnishings for private clients by hand,

I wasn't really feeling anything. I needed to do something, anything that would distract me just for moment from the devastating news that Kelly wasn't mine. News I was still trying to comprehend. I went to the local Spar shop, a familiar place, and bought beer, Carling, for myself and I'm sure a bottle of white wine, Chardonnay most likely, for Lois.

Having a drink, needing a drink, seemed to be the appropriate response for dealing with it. I didn't want to see anyone I knew for fear they'd see something was wrong, see or sense my upset. I didn't want to tell anyone anything, especially not until I'd had some time to digest it. To come to terms with it, to have a plan, know what actions I would or should take.

I remember walking past The Bricklayers pub. Sounds of jollity emanated from within and people inside were having a good time, enjoying the last moments of the weekend, the Sunday afternoon, before having to return to work the next day.

I'm sure I kept the chat in the shop to a minimum as I paid for the alcohol. I wasn't rude, just polite but un-engaging.

I walked back to the house and entered the back yard. As I did so, it started to rain. I stopped beside Lois's car, parked outside the back door, and looked up at the sky, the rain hitting my face gently.

And then I started to feel it. Tears welled up and I let them come. I was so upset, so confused, at the news, it had taken my stopping for that moment to allow myself to think and have the realisation that Kelly wasn't mine. To get over the shock. The tears lasted no more than a few moments but it had finally hit me when I least expected it to. It was like the rain had kicked it off. After a few moments, I gathered myself to enter the house.

Lois had told her parents of the result. To this day I remember Lois's dad, Mick, saying what he thought of Meg.

"She is a wicked, wicked, woman!" He stated.

Lois and I returned to the flat upstairs and I opened the beer and wine. We stood in the kitchen, drinking, and talked about what would happen next.

I decided I needed to present my findings to Meg in a controlled and neutral environment, with a third party who was not aligned to either of us, as soon as possible. I was to phone the mediation service and arrange to meet with Meg "to discuss future maintenance arrangements". It was a ploy, to hide the real nature of the meeting and one which, being around money, I was sure would get her agreement and attendance to.

And then my phone rang. It was Kelly. Oblivious to my new situation, of course, I had to maintain the status quo for her sake. I had to appear normal to her for fear of tipping Meg off about what I had discovered.

We talked about Kelly coming to see me, Lois and Brian, the dog – Kelly was always asking after the dog - the following weekend. She was so excited and it literally broke my heart to have to lie to her again as I didn't know what would be appropriate given the plan I was thinking of executing during the week preceding.

It upsets me now writing about it and I have to stop for a moment as the tears I'm crying right now are stinging my eyes.

I'd only lied to her once before, in all of her life, and that was when I took the DNA sample. If I had the chance, I'd tell her how sorry I was for lying to her, especially when we had a deal: No secrets and no lies.

After the phone call I wept, uncontrollably. Lois held me and tried to comfort me. It was so hard. I had never felt anything like it before and my body ached with every movement and I just wanted the pain to go away.

We drank some more and then retired to bed. It was going to be a long week.

*   *   *

The next morning I contacted the Reading Mediation Service and asked them if they could arrange a meeting as soon as possible between Meg and me. I told them it was absolutely critical that someone be present and that it happen at the earliest possible opportunity and I was relieved when they came back to me and said they had a place available on the 1st of August.

Meg agreed, via the mediator, to attend the lunchtime session.

Over the next day or so, I prepared exactly what I was going to say to her, writing it down to be sure of not slipping up or mis-communicating what was to be said.

*   *   *

On the day of the meeting, I arrived and was shown into a small, sparsely decorated room whilst Meg was met and brought to the room.

She sat down and the mediator indicated I should start. I started reading from the notes I'd made. I only got the opportunity to state the first paragraph:

"I will not be paying any further maintenance as I have discovered that Kelly is not mine. I have conducted a DNA test that clearly shows without doubt that I am not the father of Kelly."

I handed the mediator a copy of the results of the DNA relationship test which she passed to Meg.

Meg just laughed. She shook her head and laughed. Almost at once, her whole demeanor and reaction told me that she knew. She knew and she'd been found out. There were no proclamations of "that's not true" or "that cannot be!"

She just laughed.

"How did you get a test done? You need my permission." Meg asked.

I explained to her that, as I had parental responsibility, I didn't need her permission to conduct the test. The entire test was conducted legally. Although I hadn't notified Meg of the test, I hadn't actually done anything wrong.

Meg went on to ask about what was going to happen regarding my scheduled looking after of Kelly for that coming weekend and the subsequent two weeks. I suggested that, given the situation, it may not be appropriate for me to see Kelly until this initial situation was resolved. Meg seemed annoyed at the fact she'd have to make alternative childcare arrangements.

Meg said she needed to check the results herself, for accuracy, and take advice on the situation and the mediator led Meg out to the reception area.

I waited for a short while for the mediator to return and asked where the bathroom was. As I went to the bathroom, I saw Meg talking to her then boyfriend, Opie. A guy with tattoos on his neck, one of his own name, who looked to be somewhat angry at what Meg was telling him and the look he gave me as I crossed the corridor gave me concern for my safety.

When I returned to the mediation room, I asked the mediator if there was an alternative way out of the building rather than the front door as I was worried about repercussions, particularly from Meg's boyfriend and didn't wish there to be any further confrontation. The mediator directed me to a set of stairs which led down and to a rear entrance that allowed me a discreet exit onto the high street. I quickly made my way to my car and started my journey home.

Chapter Thirteen

Over the next few days, I was to discover that Meg had contacted Anglian DNA making accusations about how the test had been carried out and, according to the receptionist at Anglian DNA, shouting about how it had been conducted illegally.

I sent the Child Support Agency the details of the results of the test and asked them to desist from a planned assessment they were trying to make against me. The assessment was required as I had previously been making payments voluntarily. I told them that the evidence I'd enclosed with the letter established that I was "**not** the father and therefore **not** the absent parent for the purposes of the Child Support Act".

I also went on to state that "the agency has no statutory power to make any further assessment against me. If my former partner wants maintenance, she will have to apply to the family court or give you the real father's details so that you can pursue the right person."

I also requested that "all monies that have been paid directly to you [The CSA] were refunded without delay."

* * *

Two weeks later, on 13th August 2007, Loretta Brown from the Child Support Agency telephoned me. Loretta explained the reason she had rung me was because "Meg Griffin has asked them [the CSA] to collect the child maintenance."

I tried to explain to Loretta that I had sent a letter to the CSA a week before, which detailed I was not the father, but she simply refused to acknowledge this, or listen to anything I had to say, and eventually hung up on me! Such was her insistence on pursuing me for the money, she simply refused to accept I'd sent a letter.

I phoned the CSA back to try and speak to John Herbert or Stewart Gilligan. They were senior management with whom I'd previously gotten progression when there were issues. Both were unavailable. I spoke to someone called Neil Goldman – he took my number. Despite my saying it very slowly, he still managed to get it wrong. He said he would phone me back once he'd received the email I was sending him which contained copies of the letter I'd sent the week before with the evidence of non-paternity.

Later that day, Mr Goldman called me back. From his comments, it appeared he took Meg's word for everything and would not accept the evidence I'd sent him as evidence of non-paternity. It seemed I had to have the test re-taken via a doctor and Meg and Kelly would also have to have a test conducted by their doctor.

Mr Goldman told me the CSA would take maintenance money from me on the 3rd of September unless I proved by an independent and legally admissible DNA test that I was not the father. It was me that was presumed guilty of being the father before being proved innocent. It was also me that had to find the money for the test and the necessary court fees/solicitor fees to prove that I was not the father.

Mr Goldman informed me that I would get any money that the CSA took, or would take, from me back, once I proved I was not the father, but further advised there would be no compensation for the trouble or stress and illness that I suffered as a result of the CSA's continuing unfair treatment towards me. As a result of this conversation, feeling totally backed into a corner with the injustice of it all, I lost it somewhat.

"I wish I had a fucking gun because if I did I would come down there and kill all you fuckers!" I yelled and hung up.

I contacted Anglian DNA who kindly arranged for the DNA Legal Test to be sent to the relevant GP's and letters to Meg requesting her to attend her GP to have the test completed.

I was, as you can imagine, absolutely furious. I was so angry, I talked to Lois about my intention to sue Meg not only for every penny of maintenance paid, but also for all of the court fees that I incurred as a result of her refusal to acknowledge this test and for pursuing the CSA to get the money from me.

I wrote a letter and sent it to five different departments of the CSA to try and get a re-assessment arranged and a deferment of collection of the maintenance.

A week passed and I received no acknowledgement or response to my letter.

* * *

Having not heard anything back to my letters, on the 20th of August, I telephoned the CSA to try and speak to John Herbert to request details of every payment taken or received since the very first assessment and to obtain a list of approved centres for the DNA testing, as it appeared that Anglian DNA were not on the approved list.

The first woman I spoke to was in Liverpool and couldn't find John Herbert's number. I hung up and tried phoning again in the hope of getting through to someone less incompetent. I was put on hold for some time whilst the next agent tried to locate him. I gave up and tried another number. I got through to Neil Goldman again and made the request for the list of approved DNA test centres. The request was refused. The CSA (Mr Goldman) refused to send me a list of approved centres!

I told Neil Goldman that the CSA website said that the costs of the DNA test would be refunded; He confirmed this was the case and also told me he'll get me a full account breakdown by the end of that week.

Seemingly kindly, he also stated that he'd find out what assistance the CSA could give me in recovering money paid directly to Meg.

I made an application to the court for a "Declaration of Non-Parentage". This would be crucial as part of the evidence to prevent the CSA pursuing me for maintenance money. My court date was listed as 13th September 2007.

* * *

At the beginning of August 2007, I wrote to the Independent Case Examiner, as this seemed to be the initial route regarding any complaints against the CSA. I sent them details listing dozens of examples of maladministration, incorrect enforcement actions, failures to respond to correspondence adequately, mis-information and hundreds of examples of poor customer service.

Some of these examples included:

- Continual "loss" of documents/letters/paperwork/computer entries/phone records.
- Refusal to send requested assessment forms

- Refusal to send list of approved DNA centres
- Conflicting information regarding whether or not I would receive a full refund of the DNA testing I have been forced to action
- Sending of the wrong forms
- Despite telling me they [The CSA] would not contact my employer without notifying me first, they contacted my employer without my prior knowledge.
- Despite me telling them not to share any of the details of my conversations with the agency with Miss Griffin, Miss Griffin testified in court that she had been told of my manner with CSA staff.
- I was told that in order to send documents electronically, because their email service strips attachments, I'd have to go to the website and send them via the secure server. When I went to the secure server, there was no facility to send attachments.
- I wrote to the Secretary of State – the head of the DWP, but received no response.
- I wrote to Tom Tucker, the chief executive of the CSA and received no response.
- I wrote to the Complaints Departments of the CSA and received no response.
- Copies of documents, such as my bank statements and payslips that I sent to the CSA were sent to Miss Griffin.

- The CSA actually advised Miss Griffin in pursuing me for more money, and refused to assist in negotiations and to communicate my offer of maintenance to her, despite stating that they encouraged people to make agreements between themselves.
- John Herbert, who I spoke to previously, refused to speak to me stating "I have no knowledge of the case" despite him being deeply involved with my case and very helpful before. Despite trying several times to get through to him, or his colleague Mr Gilligan, no-one would put me through or even take a message.

At the end of August, I received a letter from the Independent Case Examiner that told me that my complaint related to "Child Support Legislation." My complaint clearly didn't relate to this and I again wrote to the Independent Case Examiner detailing the dozens of examples of maladministration.

At the beginning of September 2007, I received a letter from the Independent Case Examiner that informed me that they would let the CSA respond to my enquiry/complaint.

The whole point of me contacting the ICE was due to the fact that I wasn't getting any traction in pursuing my complaint against the CSA. It's only following this the ICE determined it was appropriate for the CSA to respond to my complaint!

* * *

Over the next month, the CSA stated that it hadn't received any notice of my intention to dispute paternity. In a letter dated 4th September 2007, addressed to Miss Griffin, the CSA stated "Our records do not show that this issue [my intention to dispute paternity] has been raised prior to this date."

I attended court on 13th September 2007. Judge Swanson, who presided over my case, was extremely biased against me. The judge refused to acknowledge my evidence, refused to allow me to speak, and totally failed to give me a fair hearing.

The judge suggested the way I conducted the initial testing was "reprehensible" despite the fact I hadn't done anything wrong. It may have been underhand, it may have been discreet and without consideration or notification to Meg, but it wasn't illegal.

Judge Swanson also failed to give me correct and appropriate directions in respect of the case. Had I not gotten legal advice following it, it would have resulted in my not being able to pursue my case due to it being out of time or heard at the wrong court. As a result, I specifically requested that future hearings not be with this unfair and biased woman.

Due to the issues with the case being misrouted or the wrong application being made, I decided to engage a solicitor who had experience in family matters.

*   *   *

The next day I received another letter from the ICE saying that my complaint "*does* fall into their remit."

The CSA continued to aggressively pursue me for the maintenance of nearly £600. They refused to review or suspend my assessment due to "presumed parentage".

Within a week my employer received a "Detachment of earnings" order which authorised the CSA to be paid directly from my salary the amount of any maintenance that was due.

It was my understanding that these orders usually took at least fourteen days to process. Yet this one looked as if it had been rushed through in order to inconvenience me as much as possible and not give me a reasonable time to make a payment or to get a DNA test completed in time to resolve the issue of Paternity with the CSA.

Someone from the CSA, some days following the receipt of the DOE by my employer, contacted the personnel department to confirm they had receipt of it.

Even the people in Human Resources told me it's most unusual for anyone to contact them to confirm receipt of a DOE and for one of these orders to be processed so quickly.

The HR people indicated to me that they normally took around five to six weeks.

The order detailed that more than half of my salary was to be taken as payment of maintenance, despite earlier indications it would be around one-third. The order was also flawed with major errors which, essentially, made it invalid:

- The order did not detail the type of work I did.
- The order did not detail my works number.
- The order did not detail the amount or amounts to be taken and the dates of any change to these amounts covering the following 52 weeks
- The order did not detail my protected earnings rate.

Despite this, the CSA still intended to take the money. The only recourse I had, was to take the issue to a Magistrates Court, at my own and further expense.

At the end of September I received another Detachment of Earnings Order. The new one detailed different amounts to the first one though it still said they'd take more than half of my salary!

* * *

I requested information from the CSA regarding the data they held on file in respect of me. I made this request under the Data Protection Act. I had to make the request at least four times before the data was sent to me.

The solicitor I engaged to assist in my application for a Declaration of Non Parentage had written to the CSA, informing them of the intended application being made. The CSA continued to refuse to defer the Detachment of Earnings Order. With half my salary gone in October, it made for a very hard couple of months. The CSA stated that I was doing the right thing by making the application to the court. They in fact sanctioned that I *had* to go to court.

* * *

In mid-October, I received a letter from the Independent Case Examiner that said that the CSA had "not completed its examination of [my] complaint". It went on to say that this being the case, the ICE could not progress in its consideration of my complaint.

One minute the complaint was with the ICE, the next it was with the CSA, then back to the ICE and finally again with the CSA. It was all very confusing.

* * *

On the 11th of October I wrote to the Central Appeals Unit to appeal against the DEO. For some reason, my letter was not officially received by the Agency until 23rd October 2007.

More than a week later I received a response. It told me my appeal was "outside of the jurisdiction of the Central Appeals Unit and the Tribunal Service." It further informed me I should write to my magistrates to appeal the order. This was yet more mis-information. I was previously informed, by the tribunal's service, that the procedure was to contact the agency first.

I subsequently wrote to my magistrates only to find out that I would have to pay in excess of £175.00 to the courts to start the appeal through them! I'm not given, without excessive cost to myself, an opportunity to appeal the DEO. This struck me as being severely unfair.

* * *

I attended Reading Court on 23rd November to progress the Declaration of Non Parentage.

The judge this time around was the same judge who handled the original case five years before in respect of the Parental Responsibility Order and the Contact Order and name change. He clearly remembered the previous case and was very fair.

The court ruled that Miss Griffin must co-operate in providing a DNA sample of Kelly Megan Gates and herself. I was also to provide a sample. The judge stated that if Meg didn't comply, then I could make an application for costs (which was most unusual in child cases it seems). The judge scheduled the next hearing be on 23rd January 2008 when he could sit in and conduct further proceedings given his understanding of the case etc.

We immediately made the application to CellMark (the ONLY centre it seemed the CSA would accept results from) and paid the appropriate court costs and DNA cost fees.

* * *

At the end of November I received a letter from Jonathan Weed at the CSA stating that his investigation of my complaint was ongoing but that the DEO had been withdrawn. It appeared, based on this, that the CSA *was* able to withdraw the DEO without the need for me to be referred to the magistrates' court. I cited this as further examples of incompetence and misdirection.

Meg continued to defer having the DNA test completed and the original court date for reviewing the evidence, the 23rd of January, was pushed back to 3rd March 2008.

Finally, on 28th January 2008, I received a letter from CellMark that confirmed the tests had all been completed. It again confirmed I was not Kelly's biological father.

At the end of January, I received a further letter, almost repeating a letter I received at the end of December, from the CSA, It detailed: "If you do not make payment by 4 February 2008, the Agency will look to securing payments through a new Deduction from Earnings Order". I found this severely distressing, especially given Mr Weed's knowledge of my situation at that time.

Chapter Fourteen

Whilst the battle with the CSA was going on, in late September 2007, I was contacted by Kelly's school.

They told me Kelly had been getting into fights and not being her usual self. Possibly as a consequence of being separated from me. I had no idea what Meg had told her in respect of what had happened or why I wasn't seeing her.

Not seeing her had been tremendously hard on me. I simply didn't know what to do for the best, and for her sake. It was truly terrible and on reflection I wondered if I should have carried on seeing her, knowing what I knew. I wondered what kind of effect that would have had on me and how I would explain to this little, wonderful girl how I wasn't her real father but still felt like her "Dad".

I recalled seeing an ornament at my friend Chris' house. He'd taken on Tom, when he started seeing Rachel. Tom was Rachel's only child from a previous relationship. On the ornament it said, "Anyone can be a father... But it takes someone special to be a Dad". I thought that summed it up rather well.

Everyone had told me that I was a good Dad to Kelly. Even strangers commented how patient I was. When teaching Kelly to swim, a woman came up to me and said "I don't know how you have so much patience. I would have given up a long time ago."

I told the school what had happened, about how I had discovered I wasn't Kelly's real father. The school went on to tell me that they'd talked to Kelly to find out why her behaviour had changed. Kelly had told them she missed me. She had also told them she thought I was dying or dead.

I was heartbroken. Not just for myself, but for her. To be having those kinds of thoughts must have been awful for her and it was all I could do not to break down whilst on the phone to the school. My voice stammered and tears rolled down my face.

I offered to go to the school to see Kelly, to reassure her I was okay but told the school it would be best if they contacted Meg as she would need to give her permission for me to see her.

I never heard from the school again. When I phoned a few weeks later, to check Kelly was okay, they assured me she was fine and that Meg had informed them I was not to be allowed any contact with her.

In October, I stopped off at a Tesco's store near Camberley to get some provisions on the way home. As I walked along the aisles, I saw Kelly with Meg!

"Hello Kelly." I said to her. She looked shocked and nervous and stepped closer to her mother momentarily. Meg looked scared to death!

"How are you?" I asked.

"Fine." She said timidly.

"Do I get a hug?" I asked. She stepped forward as I knelt down and gave me a hug. I didn't want to let her go.

"I'm sorry I haven't been able to see you." I said.

"That's okay." She replied.

"I did ask to see you, but your Mum said 'No'" I said.

"Lies!" Her mother said.

"What?" I looked up at Meg and stood up as she grabbed Kelly's hand and started pulling Kelly away from me.

"Lies!" Meg said again.

"You haven't told her?" I looked at her as she pushed past me and started down another aisle with me following. "I can't believe you haven't told her."

Meg was frantically dialing someone on her phone as she continued to drag Kelly away.

"I'm sorry Kelly." I said. "If your Mum's okay with it, you can phone me if you like." I said. "Do you want my number?"

"No, it's okay." Kelly said. Just before she was swept into another aisle, I called out to her one last time.

"I love you." I said.

I left the supermarket. I didn't want to create a scene in public and certainly didn't want to upset Kelly or myself any further.

I drove home with tears streaming down my face. I phoned my Mum and Dad to tell them I'd seen her. It had been especially tough on my Mum so I knew she'd be glad to have some news of Kelly.

At least having seen me, Kelly would know I wasn't dying or dead. That gave me some comfort at least.

In time for Kelly's birthday, on November 25th 2007, I sent her a card. I still felt she was my daughter, even if she wasn't biologically, and vowed I'd never forget her birthday.

On the morning of the 25th, I received a text from Meg:
25th November 2007
10.23.29 (From Meg)

Your sick!! You gave up being Kellys dad and then you send a card signed dada don't mess with Kellys head. Leave her alone, all she wants from you is her bratz dolls returned and any other belongings she has there that were from here. I'll even refund you the postage to send them back.

I never replied but realised that so many of Kelly's toys were still at mine. Over the next few months, I boxed them up and took them to her, leaving them at the front door during the day when no-one would be at home.

Chapter Fifteen

Despite Meg's delaying tactics in respect of having the DNA testing completed, Lois and I and a solicitor acting as my counsel on behalf of my solicitor finally attended court at the beginning of March 2008.

Whilst waiting for our hearing, I noticed that the judge on the case was not the same as that we had previously on 23rd November, or as scheduled for the 23rd January date.

To my horror it was Judge Swanson. I immediately brought this to the attention of my counsel who raised the issue with the desk staff stating that the previous judge had specifically directed he should hear this case.

The receptionist highlighted the fact that due to the 23rd January date being deferred to the 3rd of March and the original judge not being available, Judge Swanson was to hear it. We asked for a further deferment but were refused. Given my previous experience with Judge Swanson, I felt doomed. I knew it would not be a fair hearing again.

Even with my being represented by counsel, I knew that we were not going to be able to present our case and have it heard fairly in an un-biased fashion and without prejudice.

As expected, Judge Swanson was aggressive from the start. She showed scant regard for the actual case details and refused to respect mine or my counsel's views and evidence on the case.

Judge Swanson actually made the accusation that I had obtained Parental Responsibility in order to obtain a DNA test without the mother's permission. Even when my counsel pointed out that the Parental Responsibility Order was obtained some four years before, Judge Swanson still refused to accept that the court proceedings were un-necessary. She absolutely refused to accept that we were only there as it was the only choice I had due to the lack of co-operation by the respondent, Meg Griffin.

Judge Swanson also refused to grant me costs, which would have almost certainly been made due to Meg forcing me to court.

I lost my temper and told the judge what I thought of her decision. I told her that the mother lied for seven years and destroyed a relationship between a dad and his daughter whilst she gets away with her lie with zero consequences.

I was absolutely raging, ranting. My counsel sat quietly, whilst I let loose and vented my anger at the unfair behaviour of this "judge". Eventually, I left the room and tried to calm myself down outside the open door.

I heard the judge speak to my counsel.

"May I remind you," she told him, "Your client is in contempt of court."

I reeled back into the entrance of the chambers. I shouted at her stating my feelings on the injustice of it all. I tried to explain, through my rage and disappointment, that the only reason I was in contempt is because of the judges' refusal to give me and my counsel a fair hearing. I was absolutely livid. I found myself shaking violently with the stress and emotional trauma of it all.

The judge told my counsel after I left for the second time that she wouldn't pursue the matter of the contempt.

I met Lois in reception. I was visibly shaking with the rage of it all. I don't think I'd ever been so angry in all my life.

My counsel joined us and I apologised for my outburst. Meg and her mother had already left which was probably just as well.

"It's fine," he said calmly, "I didn't say anything because you were right." I felt somewhat exonerated for my reaction to the judge.

I was, and still am, utterly appalled and disgusted that someone who was so unfair and biased could be in the position she holds.

Despite all of this, we were granted a Declaration of non-Paternity.

This case was needlessly brought before the court due to the fact that the mother refused to co-operate with an official DNA test and left me with **no other option** but to bring the matter to court to resolve. The fact that the judge refused to accept this and actually stated that the reason for not giving costs was because I had acted reprehensibly in the manner at which I obtained the first DNA test result suggested that she had no interest in making a fair and impartial decision based on the evidence before her and led me to issue a formal complaint against her.

The complaint was never upheld. The Office for Judicial Complaints suggested that the judge was "entitled to express his or her opinion". Despite the facts that, on two occasions, Judge Swanson demeaned my counsel and refused to listen or show acknowledgement to the overwhelming evidence we presented, no action or disciplinary procedures were taken against her with the Office stating they "did not find that what District Judge said was outside the bounds of courtesy".

The Office for Judicial Complaints referred my letter of complaint to Judge Swanson for her comments. Mysteriously, the Court Manager was "unable to locate the tape of the 13th September hearing."

The office went on to state "a Judge is obliged by the Judicial Oath to exercise his/her judicial functions without "fear, or favour, affection or ill-will" and that if a litigant/defendant feels that the situation has, for whatever reason, been assessed wrongly, the only recourse is to appeal."

Of course, an appeal would have only cost me further money and my counsel advised me that it stood only a fifty-fifty chance of being changed. Not the best odds.

In respect of the judge failing to give me correct and appropriate directions and what evidence is allowed or disallowed, the Office for Judicial Complaints dismissed my complaint.

The Office acknowledged they knew I would "be disappointed by their response". This only went to suggest they didn't feel it fair either.

Chapter Sixteen

After the court case, I needed time to calm down. Lois didn't want me to drive in the state I was in and we decided to take a walk around Reading town centre.

Meg had been at court with her mother and they'd both left the court building whilst I was having my argument with the judge.

We walked into one of the shopping malls and I saw them in one of the shops. I directed myself and Lois away and we took another route away from them.

Bizarrely, we ended up running into them again in another clothing shop and this time I wasn't able to take any action in time to avoid a confrontation.

Lois wanted to take Meg to task.

"Are you spending the real father's money now?" Lois shouted at Meg.

They didn't even look at us. Clearly embarrassed.

I told Lois that no matter what we should maintain our dignity.

"Come on, let's go." I said.

I wished afterwards that I'd let Lois fully confront Meg. For months Lois had watched me go through hell. She'd lived my pain with me. She watched and experienced the hurt I felt as I broke down with the "loss" of Kelly from my life. She had been with me as I became an emotional wreck, missing Kelly day-to-day. She had supported me tremendously but, warranted, it had been difficult for her to cope with too.

Meg had suffered no consequence for her actions. She'd lied for seven years and there'd been no comeback against her for it. She didn't seem to be remorseful or regretful in any way.

And I think Lois needed something, anything, to get some kind of payback for what Meg had put me through. Even if no good could have come of it, a part of me later wished Lois had smacked the bitch and smacked her hard.

Even my friends wondered why Meg, who must have had some doubt as to my being the father, had given me such a hard time about money in particular over so many years.

"Surely she'd want to keep you sweet during that whole time?" My mate Debbie said when reflecting over the events.

I dragged Lois from the store and we drove home stopping at a country pub to get something to eat and have a drink. It wasn't a very enjoyable meal. The food and drink was fine but the whole day had left a bad taste in our mouths.

Chapter Seventeen

Immediately following the court case my solicitor sent the CSA's Office of the Solicitor the Declaration of Non Paternity and requested cancellation of the CSA assessment and asked for a refund of all payments made with interest thereon. A claim for the costs associated with obtaining the DNA test and Declaration of Non Paternity, which we were instructed to action by the CSA themselves, was also made.

One month later, as a result of not hearing anything, I phoned the CSA's Office of the Solicitor to try and get progression. Within a few days, my solicitor received a letter from the CSA's Office of the Solicitor. It detailed the CSA had closed my file and that the arrears of child maintenance had been adjusted to nil.

Later that month, I heard from Mr Adam West at the CSA. He informed me that Jonathan Weed no longer worked for the agency. Mr West explained that he needed another day to come to a decision regarding the repayment that my solicitor had written about and would write to me thereafter.

Several days passed. I heard nothing from Mr West; I phoned the CSA complaints office. The line rang and rang with no-one answering. I tried for more than an hour. I phoned the office of the solicitor. She told me she was due to write a letter to my solicitor stating that the CSA will pay me back the money I paid to them that was passed onto the PWC (Parent with Care, Meg Griffin). She detailed this total to be £2137.28. It seemed there was no mention of the costs associated with the DNA Test being refunded.

I tried a different number for Mr West and got through to him. He explained that there was the possibility, as in certain cases there was a dispensation for it, that I could be paid back not only the money I paid to the CSA but also the money I paid to the Parent with Care directly. However, he went on to say that he needed to check with the policy people as it seemed they may have mis-interpreted him. He went on to ask me to call back the next day when he would be at his desk so that he could give me a committed answer.

I informed my solicitor that if a letter came stating only the CSA payments of £2137.28 were being refunded to respond detailing that the CSA had – via their website and directly through a conversation I'd had with Neil Goldman back in August – committed to refunding the costs of getting a DNA test completed.

On 22nd April, I phoned Mr West. He detailed that I would be getting back all of the money paid directly to Miss Griffin. He quoted me a figure of "around £13,000". When I queried this, as my figure was closer to £20,000, he stated "I don't have the exact figure to hand but it will be all of it".

I also asked him about the money for the DNA test and associated costs. He said "Let's get the money you paid back to you and then we can process that separately". He asked how I would like the money paid; "via bank draft or directly into my bank account." I told him straight into my bank account was preferable and supplied him with my bank details. He said he'd get this processed as soon as possible as he knew I'd "been waiting a long time for things to be sorted out."

The following day, 23rd April 2008, The Department for Work and Pensions wrote to my solicitor. The letter stated that only £2,137.28 (payments made directly to the Agency) would be refunded. The letter went on to state that as the "DNA testing was instigated by Mr Gates and not at the request of the Agency… the Agency [was] not liable to pay the cost of the DNA test". The CSA refused to assist me in obtaining a DNA test. They refused to send me a list of test centres. They instructed me to obtain, via a court, a Declaration of Non Paternity. The CSA told me, when I began the process that I was "doing the right thing". They also, via Neil Goldman's comments in August (and on the CSA's website), stated that I would be refunded the costs associated with obtaining the DNA test. To declare that they were not party to the application, despite being invited by my solicitor to be, was absurd.

A week went by. I phoned Adam West. Again he confirmed I would be getting back all the money I had paid directly to Miss Griffin. I detailed to him that the letter I had received said something different. Adam informed me he'd noticed this last week and that it had been too late to stop the letter going out. He said he'd raise it with the policy team as it was "not that which I [Adam West] suggested we recompense you with." Adam promised he'd get back to me later that day or first thing the next.

Two days later, my solicitor wrote a long letter[2] to the DWP contesting their allegations and refusal to refund me in full.

The letter highlighted the fact that Adam West said I'd be getting all the money I had paid back on at least two occasions. My solicitor broke down all of the funds paid between April 2000 and July 2007, which totalled £22,865.88.

The CSA were also informed of the confusion that had been created by the suggestions from Mr West around my being told one thing one day and another the next which contradicted that which had been said before.

My solicitor also requested the legal costs back too and detailed that I had been forced to go to court because the CSA were not willing to accept the results that I had presented. It was further highlighted to the CSA that they had confirmed my going to court was "the right thing to do".

The fact that their own website detailed costs of DNA tests where the non-resident parent is found not to be the father would be reimbursed was also referenced.

---

[2] See Appendix Two for full letter written to the Department of Work and Pensions.

The grand total requested by the letter was £29,154.49.

* * *

A month passed with nothing from the CSA. Finally, on 29th May 2008 we received a response from the Department of Work and Pensions. The letter said that Mr West "did not tell your client that he would be reimbursed". This was an absolute lie and I'm glad I had transcripts of telephone conversations I made and recordings that detail he did.

The letter went on to state that as this was an "old scheme" case, there was no statutory basis for the Agency to reimburse voluntary payments.

The fact this was an "old scheme" case was irrelevant and I felt I should not be treated differently to someone on a "new scheme" case, whereby – by inference – the suggestion was that if I were on a new scheme I *would* be reimbursed.

The letter also stated the Agency did not receive confirmation from the PWC that the voluntary/direct payments were in lieu of child maintenance. I contested this and referred directly to the letter to the CSA in which Miss Griffin clearly indicated the private arrangement *was* for child maintenance payments.

I explained to Mr West that every step of the way the CSA were made aware of my payments directly to Miss Griffin.

This was borne out by the fact that in a letter from them, dated 28th December 2007, they acknowledged the payments as coming off of my balance.

The CSA were continuously made aware of any arrangements between me and Miss Griffin – otherwise, why would they have pursued me for the outstanding maintenance?

I told Mr West that I had been "consistently lied to", to which he responded saying "I just misread the legislation."

I explained to him that he shouldn't be misreading anything. I reiterated that on two separate occasions he'd told me I'd be getting all of the money back that I'd paid to Miss Griffin". He argued that he'd said "possibly, not definitely" and I told him again, "You told me I would be getting ALL of it back."

I referred to the conversation I had with him the day before. "You said yesterday that the information in the letter was not in line with what your suggestion was to the policy team. You said that I was getting all of the money back yesterday." I repeated that "I've been lied to and lied to and lied to."

The letter went on to reverse the decision made regarding the cost of the DNA test but not the costs associated with obtaining it – despite my being assured by Neil Goldman this would be the case. It also suggested the agency "acted entirely properly."

I didn't believe for one second the agency acted "entirely properly". They had consistently said one thing to me one day, another to me the next. They had contradicted their own rules/guidance by offsetting direct payments against my balance but refused to refund these as it suited them to do so.

I also believed that some significant form of financial redress for maladministration should be forthcoming due to the sustained and ongoing incompetence and delays I had to suffer at their hands. In the CSA's own words, I should have received a payment "**if our action or lack of action caused: serious inconvenience as a result of repeated mistakes**." Also, from the DWP website: the following justifications for maladministration were clear: "**neglect, inattention, delay, incompetence, ineptitude**"

Mr. West directly admitted his incompetence in misreading the legislation. Also, from the Ombudsman website: "**Maladministration generally means poor administration or the wrong application of rules**".

Further to this, my fiancée, Lois, suffered severely due to the stress caused by the CSA's actions. As a result she went to see her doctor and, after breaking down in tears in his surgery and explaining what had been going on, she was placed on medication.

The relationship between Lois and me also suffered significantly during this period due directly to the stress. Finding out Kelly, who for seven and a half years I'd seen as my daughter, wasn't mine was hard enough to deal with on its own. I was considerably upset at the discovery as you might imagine and, even now, still get upset at the events and loss I suffered. On a personal level, being reminded of things I did with her, whether it be whilst watching television or being a part of something, is extremely upsetting. Lois found some photos of Kelly with Brian on her camera that I never even knew she'd taken. Despite being out-of-focus, I broke down in tears when I saw them.

Having to deal with and fight against the CSA whose lack of compassion, understanding, empathy and willingness to assist me in this circumstance beggared belief, was something that caused a great deal of distress and upset. Being subjected to significant financial hardship by having more than 50% of my salary deducted at source at a time when I was expected to fund court costs and DNA testing costs, just added to the stress.

As a result, I requested that all my direct payments to Miss Griffin and all payments made to the CSA, along with the costs for the DNA Testing and all costs associated with having to obtain a DNA test the CSA would accept be refunded without delay. The total came to £29,154.49 and was detailed in my solicitor's letter of 30th April 2008 to the CSA.

I also asked that an interest payment on the total be made in addition to this to cover that which I would not have lost had I been able to invest the money elsewhere.

Finally, in the CSA's letter, we were directed to the Financial Redress for Maladministration Guide and asked if we would like to apply for a special payment. Despite applying for this by contacting the Agency as suggested in their letter, we got no response.

*   *   *

A month later, at the end of June 2008, the CSA sent me a cheque. It was only for £2137.28 and not for the full amount that they previously said they'd pay me back.

The letter accompanying the cheque suggested this was "compensation". This is in fact only the money I paid **directly** to the CSA and it was without interest. To call it "compensation" when it was money that was rightfully mine was downright insulting.

Chapter Eighteen

Once the court case had completed, I dropped off the final box containing Kelly's toys, clothes and other things that belonged to her. I did as I had done previously, driving to her house and leaving them outside the front door during the day when she was at school and her mother's car wasn't present outside.

Very late that day, I received a text from Meg.

16th April 2008
22.01.14 (From Meg)
Please stop leaving toys and letters for Kelly. It upset her. You stopped seeing and speaking to her that wasn't my decision. You could have done this differently. I've not painted a bad picture of you so please don't make out I've stopped you seeing her. I don't care what the test said you are her dad and since mediation she has lost you and your family. I had no say in that. Whats done is done all I ask is you let Kelly move on in her own life.

To me, that suggested that Meg recognised that I was Kelly's "Dad". I felt there was a chance for me to establish the relationship I had with Kelly and continue playing a role in her life. It would be different, but there's no reason why it couldn't be.

I sent a text back the following day.

17th April 2008

07.54.31 (From me)

Then let her see me. It would be good for her.

The conversation continued via text:

16.22.34 (From Meg)

Good for her or you? She's needs stability and at the moment she has that at home. The hardest thing was convincing her I wasn't going to leave her. You cant do the same.

17.17.28 (From me)

Having me seeing her would be good for her. I never wanted not to. She would benefit a lot from it.

19.54.57 (From Meg)

How? You cant put her down and pick her up when you choose. Think about her.

20.39.54 (From me)

I am thinking about her. This is not about me. I hoped this aspect could have been sorted a long time ago but it wasn't. It's her that matters. Nothing else.

20.52.54 (From Meg)

Then why stop seeing and speaking to her?!

07.15.40 (From me)
At the time I thought it was for the best. I was wrong. Let's not to n fro. It's your decision. It's her happiness. Let me know and we'll sort something out.

I didn't get a response. I decided to wait to let my offer to be a part of Kelly's life again to sink in. Meg would probably want to discuss it with her family. After a few weeks, I decided to see what Meg's decision was. I sent her a text again.
12th May 2008
12.25.52 (From me)
I guess the lack of response re. contact means Kelly won't be given the opportunity to see me. I think that is a shame as it would be of benefit to her.

12.30.54 (From Meg)
Kelly given the opportunity? Benefit to her? This is a childs life you have turned up side down for nearly a year. You chose to act selfishly with room for movement. Now you change your mind over text… You think im trusting you with her?!

I was angry at the suggestion this was somehow all my fault.

12.34.26 (From me)

It is your fault this occurred. Let's not forget who lied for 7 years and caused the situation to develop the way it did once your lie was found out.

12.59.29 *(From Meg)*

Keep playing the victim card… you did this. You walked away, you weren't pushed. I thought this was about whats best for Kelly?! Goodbye dave.

13.15.36 (From me)

It is about what is best 4 her. Me, Kelly and my family r victims in this as a result of ur lie. I was offering 2 be there 4 her as 2 b denied access to me will do her more harm long term. At least I tried. Does Kelly even know the truth? I suspect not. But she will one day. Do you even know who the real father is? At least when she is older I can show her I tried and that it was your choice not mine. Goodbye.

13.31.00 *(From Meg)*

My lie? Lets not forget who was cheating and split us up. I never cheated on you! Kelly knows everything thanks. You fought to prove your nothing to her so be nothing. In the long run its best for her anyway. She knows not to rely on you. Leave us alone and let her live her life.

It was incredible. Even after all that occurred, Meg was blaming me for everything that had gone wrong in her life. It was almost as if she took no responsibility for her actions whatsoever. I had never cheated on Meg. Not once. It was as if she was projecting her own guilt about what had happened onto me.

13.38.13 (From me)
You never cheated? If that were so the tests wud have shown I was the father. I never cheated on u. End of. I didn't prove I was nothing to Kelly. I only proved your lie. You had ur chance to do the right thing. Maybe u can screw the real father over if you even know who it is.

13.51.53 (From Meg)
You did all this to prove me wrong?... I hope it was worth it. Just shows how little Kelly means to you.

She really didn't get it. Meg really didn't understand why I had done what I'd done. This had been nothing to do with Kelly. Kelly was my world. She was just an innocent little girl caught up and affected by her mother's lie.

14.04.07 (From me)
Don't even begin to think you know what Kelly means to me. I did what was right. I wasn't prepared to live a lie even if u

were. At least I tried to do right by her. Don't text again unless you're prepared to do the same.

14.16.55 *(From Meg)*
Im here for her and always will be, no matter what. You went about this all wrong and you know it. Leave us alone.

14.27.01 *(From me)*
Keep thinking that way. The fact you buried your head in the sand when you were found out just demonstrates how poorly you handled this. At least I tried. Kelly will know the whole truth one day and you will have to live with the consequences of denying her access to the person she's known as her dad so far. This is your mess. Your fault. My conscience is clear. Kelly will see that. I will make sure of it.

14.31.20 *(From Meg)*
My head is held high thanks. Don't treaten me, don't contact me, and don't come to my house. Live your life and leave us to live ours. Move on dave.

14.40.20 *(From me)*
LOL. Head held high? You have no shame or sorrow for what you have done. The lies you told. The pain you caused. I guess someone who doesn't know who the real father is can afford 2 deny her daughter for now. The time will come when

Kelly will know the truth. It's not a threat. It's a promise. Goodbye.

14.42.58 (From Meg)
And this is your way of showing me you should see her... You will never get near her again.

I texted back one final time telling her she was wrong and that time would tell. I was never going to find out who the father was, though I had some suspicions.

Meg had lied to me about being in contact with a guy she knew called Glenn. Glenn had frequently "been around" even when Meg and I were seeing each other. She had assured me he was just a friend and I had no reason to think differently at the time. Meg had even been accused of having an affair with Glenn by some of her friends.

Whilst she was at mine shortly after we'd moved into the house in Fareham, she was taking a shower when her phone pinged to indicate she'd received a text message. I looked at it and it saw it was from Glenn. It was obvious from the content that they had seen each other within the last week. I deleted it.

When she came down from her shower, I casually asked her if she'd heard from him lately. She lied directly to my face and told me she hadn't heard or seen him in months.

If Glenn was the father then I could understand why she had told me I was Kelly's father. Glenn was married with two children, both girls I think, so to reveal him as the father would have meant the break-up of his marriage most likely. I was in a good job, well paid, so if she'd had to choose, I could understand why she chose me over him to "be" Kelly's Dad.

It's all conjecture though. It could have been anyone. A one-night stand, an ex-boyfriend, someone new in her life. Maybe one day I'd find out. But given that Meg kept it a secret, and would have continued to do so had she not been found out, I doubt I ever would.

Chapter Nineteen

At the end of August 2008, I decided it was time for the Parliamentary Ombudsman to get involved. Continuing with my solicitor was costing me more and more money and given I was dealing with a government agency, I discovered that the Parliamentary Ombudsman was a resource for pursuing significant dissatisfaction with one of the government's offices without it incurring any costs – or at least none that were significant.

I wrote to them and they determined, initially, that the case needed to be referred to the Independent Case Examiner (ICE) and then, if no joy, referred back to the Parliamentary Ombudsman.

ICE, it seemed, had the ability to offer compensation or redress. I wasn't hopeful, given my previous experiences with the ICE, that they would be effective in examining, reviewing and commenting on the case. Their association with the CSA being one which tended to be biased towards the CSA, not to mention the incompetence in the way they handled complaints, didn't bode well.

That said, there was little I could do but follow the process and the Parliamentary Ombudsman confirmed they were referring the case to the ICE. I wondered if the complaint was coming from the ombudsman, if there might have been a better and more favourable response.

Seven weeks later, I received a letter from the ICE.

The examiner had totally failed to grasp the basis of my complaint which was in respect of maladministration. Furthermore, they gave me just five days to respond to their letter otherwise the complaint would "time out". I found it incredulous that it took them a month to respond to any letter I sent yet they required a response from me within just five days!

Fortunately, their letter arrived mid-way through my holiday, when I was out of the country and unable to respond, and not at the start or it. If it had arrived the day after I'd left the country, my complaint would have "timed out". Maybe that was the ICE's intention?

The ICE directed me to contact the CSA in respect of providing evidence relating to my complaint when my complaint already detailed the issues of maladministration within the CSA!

I responded to them detailing they had all the evidence as previously submitted to the Parliamentary Ombudsman. I went on to state that the documentation provided by myself from the Ombudsman clearly detailed the numerous examples of **neglect, inattention, delay, incompetence, ineptitude mis-information, poor administration or the wrong application of rules, and the CSA's action or lack of action**

that in turn caused serious inconvenience as a result of repeated mistakes.

I re-iterated to them that I had no choice due to the CSA's refusal to assist me when I presented them with the initial DNA evidence, but to engage with a solicitor and take Miss Griffin (referred to in their letter as Mrs A.) to court to obtain the evidence or declaration of non-paternity that the CSA would accept. In fact, I engaged with a solicitor and took Miss Griffin to court and the CSA **confirmed and advised** that I was indeed doing the right thing by doing so.

They also requested a copy of the GP report that detailed my fiancée's severe distress. I told them I also had to have counselling earlier in the year as a result of the dealings with CSA and the resultant stress and asked them if they would like me to put them in touch with the counselling service to corroborate and provide evidence that I attended. I also told them in my response that I should like the fact I had to attend counselling to also feature, along with my fiancée's stress, as part of the financial redress.

Over the next few months, the ICE, despite having their own errors pointed out to them, just dismissed my comments and observations. The bias towards the CSA re-surfaced as they refused to acknowledge complaint after complaint.

In desperation, I wrote to them highlighting the issues in bright, blue and bold text and even commented that by doing so hopefully someone would make an attempt to understand the complaint.

They also attempted to avoid communication by letter – presumably to "hide" any incompetence made – requesting a phone call to discuss the matter. I insisted all communications were done by letter to avoid any potential misunderstandings.

Eventually, after a month of back-and-forth, they finally seemed to grasp the basis of my complaint.

On 25th November 2008 – curiously, Kelly's birthday – I received, from the CSA, a copy of an old assessment from January 2007. It was another demand for maintenance. This demand for maintenance was extremely distressing not only because it should never have been sent, but because it arrived on my *daughter's* birthday which was a very painful time for me given the circumstances. I also believed that someone, quite possibly at the CSA, was having a laugh at my expense and that's why I received this maintenance assessment at this particular time.

In December 2008, I was informed by the ICE that the CSA had been unresponsive to the ICE's requests for information. I appreciated the nightmare they were having in dealing with the CSA. I'd had to deal with them for eight years and, as was clearly documented in just one year's worth of difficulties in my complaint to the ICE, I knew what they had been going through.

The ICE detailed they were escalating to get the CSA to provide the requested information.

In January 2009 I wrote to the ICE again, as I'd heard nothing over Christmas and several weeks into the New Year.

Three months later I was again asked for information already supplied. The ICE were asking for me to provide the GP letter in relation to Lois's stress and medication. I resent the information previously sent along with the details of who to contact to confirm my attendance at counselling.

I wrote again in June asking for an update to the case. I was told the report was "imminent". I was also told that the ICE was still awaiting information from the CSA.

In July, I still hadn't heard anything and wrote again requesting an update.

On 29th July, more than a year after the original request was passed from the Ombudsman to the ICE, I received a report from Mr James Woods at the ICE. In all dealings for the last twelve months I'd been communicating with someone called Ollie Williams so to receive the report from someone other than him was bewildering.

The report they'd sent was full of numerous inconsistencies, contradictions and definitive errors and contained a complete ignorance of several specific details of my complaint. In addition to this, the bias shown in favour of the CSA was simply astounding.

I had physical evidence that simply could not be ignored yet they had seemingly chosen to gloss over my records, diary and evidence in favour of the CSA's "word". They also made personal comments in respect of events and actions outside of the CSA or ICE's jurisdiction. These comments were particularly worrying and I informed them by response that I would be requesting the Parliamentary Ombudsman take a look at the investigation as I believed it was severely flawed. It was biased and poorly-handled in much the same way as the CSA had in their dealings with me, particularly over the two years since I notified them that I was not the father of Kelly. Either that or the ICE were as incompetent as the CSA.

Even in their letter, they commented that "Specifically, you have not disputed you accepted paternity of this child for years after the child's birth." Of course I didn't! I only found out Kelly was not mine after seven and a half years! I had no reason to dispute paternity prior to this. It was clear that they didn't even understand the situation, let alone have the ability to conduct a fair and just investigation.

The letter[3] I wrote to them, detailing their mistakes and contradictions, along with my general observations, was eleven pages long!

The report had taken a year to complete, six months longer than I was originally told it would take, yet didn't even refer to a number of items in my original complaint. The

---

[3] See Appendix Three for full letter written to the Independent Case Examiner.

general feeling I had was that the report had been cobbled together in a matter of days.

Some of that delay was down to the CSA not providing information when requested to by the ICE.

The report was littered with numerous errors. The first nineteen items in the report were factually incorrect. I found it astounding that it was nineteen points into their report until I found something I agreed with or that was wholly accurate.

It was a further six items after the two items I agreed with, that were incorrect also. Some of the comments, such as "I found no evidence that you raised a paternity dispute" were plainly ridiculous. Letters referred to *earlier* in the report showed the CSA acknowledged my dispute.

The ICE also suggested that I had waited seven-and-a-half years before contesting paternity. This was nonsense of course. I didn't wait at all. I simply discovered Kelly wasn't mine and upon doing so subsequently raised the paternity dispute with them. I explained to them that I had no cause prior to this to dispute that Kelly was not mine.

The ICE referred to policy and provisions that were clearly ignored or abused. They suggested the Detachment of Earnings Order had been cancelled by Meg when, in fact, the order had been cancelled by Jonathan Weed.

The report continually repeated, contradicted and inconsistently reported across fifty items listed.

In the end, and in light of this, I decided to refer the case to the Parliamentary Ombudsman.

Out of all of the things detailed in the report, the thing that disturbed me most about the handling of the complaint was the reference to how I conducted the initial DNA test. The ICE's comment as to "serious concerns about the manner in which this test was carried out at your instigation" was nothing to do with them or my complaint at all. They brought a personal view and inference into it and whilst it may be considered reprehensible, under-hand, sneaky, or however else it might be viewed, I still had not done anything illegal.

Out of fifty listed items in the report, it was staggering to find so many inaccurate, false and just plain ridiculous comments from them. To only find a handful of the observations agreeable or without contention showed the ICE process and examination was severely flawed.

It further confirmed that the ICE was entirely biased towards the CSA and it made me shudder to think that someone like them was responsible for an investigation. All I wanted was a fair and just investigation. It was clear I did not receive such given the huge number of factual errors and inconsistencies I highlighted in my response to their investigation. The fact that they then chose just to sweep aside my comments in respect of the severely flawed report was tantamount to insult.

It made me wonder if any complaints against the CSA were upheld, given its officer's behaviour in particular.

I did not hear from the CSA in respect of any compensation and doubted I would despite the report detailing I should.

I told the ICE there would be no further correspondence in respect of this issue from myself as I requested the Ombudsman to investigate their methods and inability to conduct the investigation fairly and without bias.

Chapter Twenty

Following the court case, there were consequences for me that ran deeper than the stress that I suffered with my dealings with the CSA.

I noticed a change in my behaviour, specifically when at work one day and having to deal with a member of staff at my bank over the phone.

I was angry at them. They weren't listening to me or were failing entirely in understanding what I was trying to communicate to them regarding some spurious charges that had appeared on my account.

In a loud and clearly agitated voice, I said to the bank clerk, "You're hearing me but you're not listening to me!"

There was an audible gasp and "Oh" from the people in my team sat at their desks around me.

This wasn't me. This wasn't who I was. I was so normally calm and controlled in situations like this. Having had to deal with the stress of handling and managing the CSA's incompetence had clearly started to take its toll.

That and coming to terms with losing Kelly, grieving to some degree, was having an effect on my well-being and demeanour.

Lois had always said, "If we can get through this, we'll be able to get through anything."

I decided to get some counselling. Because it had come from me, Lois felt it was a good thing. A recognition of my needing help to come to terms with things.

I initially spoke to someone over the phone via my employer's health-care company and as a result of that discussion it was agreed that I should attend the counsellor's office the following week for a full session.

The session was only an hour long but during it I explained everything that had occurred. I wept when doing so. Apart from my parents, family, Lois and close friends, I'd not really spoken about the events to anyone else. And certainly not to a stranger.

I arranged a follow-up session a week later. Two-thirds of the way through that session I felt sharing my experience with someone I didn't know to be therapeutic and felt quite different and uplifted by the counselling. I deemed at that point that I was happy and more positive and cancelled the remaining sessions and cut short the second one.

Lois and I then took a holiday. We just needed to get away, just needed to be by ourselves and away from all the noise and stress of the CSA and everything else.

We flew to Gran Canarias and spent a week in the sun. When we were on holiday, I would keep a diary of events and experiences to look back on at a later date.

Lois even contributed to one. Her entry on June 1st 2008 read:

"Bullshit aside, this holiday is a winner. It has re-affirmed my love for David and now we will go forward with a newer and clearer future."

It seemed the holiday was just what we needed. We would score the holiday's aspects to determine logically if it was a good or bad holiday. I scored it 76% and Lois scored it 79%. A definite success.

Over the course of the next year, it became obvious I still hadn't come to terms with things fully. I had moments of extreme anger which was most unlike me. I was drinking more and failing to make an effort in restoring myself back to who I was previously both physically and mentally. My weight also spiraled.

The strain on my relationship with Lois only increased. She started to find me unattractive as I gained weight. And then there was the debt.

I got myself onto a debt management plan to manage my outstanding debt legacy from when I had sold the house after finding out that myself and Lois wouldn't be able to buy a new place together. Only when I confronted the debt did I realise the full extent of it. It was about fifty per-cent more than I thought it was originally. An absolutely horrendous amount.

Getting on the debt management plan was something I wished I'd done years before. It was one of the best things I ever did as it gave me back control over my finances and stopped the harassment I was getting from credit card and loan companies.

However, it was too little too late. Finding out how much the total debt was left Lois aghast. It created more strain despite the fact I was putting things right.

In June 2009, exactly one year after Lois declared we had a better future, I moved out of the flat above her parents that we shared into my own flat in Bournemouth. We were arguing about small, trivial and inconsequential things and I made the decision to leave. I think Lois was relieved.

On the day I moved, I told Lois it was the beginning of the end.

"Within six months," I told her, "We'll be over." She disagreed.

"I think this could even be good for us." She told me. We were no longer engaged though were still boyfriend and girlfriend. I felt that was the start of the separation really. It made no sense to me that we weren't engaged any more. Lois felt we would only get engaged if I started changing things.

My moving out would give Lois her independence back. Whilst we continued to see each other and the arguments stopped, things were not the same as they were before. Lois would, as a result of her parents selling the house, move into her own flat. This confirmed her independence even further and, whilst hard, showed her she could just about manage things, financially, on her own.

I got further counselling. A full six sessions over a period of three months. I didn't enjoy the first couple, because I didn't really feel comfortable with the counsellor and nearly cancelled but I stuck with it for the sake of my own sanity and to prove to Lois I was mending things.

It turned out the counsellor was brilliant. She helped me reveal to myself the grief I needed to experience. The closure I had to have which was denied to me in the same way that someone who has a close friend or relative that dies gets. Because I was just shut-out of Kelly's life, I didn't get any form of closure. And it was that which I had struggled most to comprehend and come to terms with.

Chapter Twenty-One

Over the next month or so, I collated everything together and constructed a full diary to send to the Parliamentary Ombudsman to review the complaint against the CSA and, further to this, the Independent Case Examiner (ICE).

It was a painful process having to "re-live" everything. I had several phone calls with the Ombudsman and spent several days scanning letters received from the CSA and ICE, sending them along with the recordings of phone calls made to the CSA to complete the mountain of evidence.

In November 2009, just ahead of Kelly's tenth birthday, I wrote to Meg asking if I could see Kelly and demonstrating my appreciation as to why she took the actions she did when Kelly was born.

Dear Meg,

I trust you and Kelly are well.

It has been a long time since I found out Kelly was not my biological daughter. Despite this, the love and attachment I had for her is still very much with me. I think about her almost constantly every single day and still consider myself to be her "dad" and to have been her father throughout the time before. Even now, after all this time, I still call her my daughter when I refer to her.

It was never my intention to stop seeing her and I realise I shouldn't have allowed that to happen. At the time I felt unsure of what to do for the best and, in hindsight, I fear that not seeing her was the wrong action to take.

It has been the hardest time of my life not seeing her, not being with her, and not having any contact with her. I'm sure it's not been easy on her either and I feel that maybe now, as she approaches her tenth birthday, that it might be a good time to put the past behind us and try and re-establish some form of contact. I'm sure Kelly has lots of questions around what has happened.

I appreciate now that you did what you did at the time for a variety of reasons and whilst I may not understand the whys and wherefores, I wouldn't seek to blame you for any of those decisions you made in Kelly's interests at the time or since. As I said, I would like to put the past behind us and move forward to do whatever we can to help Kelly. I think now would be a good time and we could use this as an opportunity to make reuniting with me an ideal present for her tenth birthday.

I hope that somewhere you will find the compassion to allow me and my family to see Kelly again. We all miss her tremendously. It has been especially hard on my Mum and I hope you can find it within you to let the past be put behind us. I am here and ready to work with you and would welcome the opportunity to discuss it with you. I'm happy to arrange mediation if you feel this would help.

I hope to hear from you soon.

David.

  I didn't get a response. I sent Kelly a birthday card with some photos of us together along with a letter to arrive on her birthday.

Dear Kelly,

HAPPY BIRTHDAY!!

I hope you have a wonderful tenth birthday. I was hoping I could see you on your birthday but I have not heard anything back from your mum who I wrote to last week asking if I could see you.

I know it has been a long time since I last saw you but I think about you every day and I would very much like to see you and have contact with you again. I miss you so very, very much. I'm sure you miss me too.

Nanny and Grampy would also love to see you as they miss you so much too. They talk about you all the time whenever I see them.

It would be lovely if you could write to me, email me or phone me. It would be so nice to hear from you.

I hope to hear from you soon.

In the meantime, have a very lovely tenth birthday. I hope you like the photos.

Lots of Love.

A short time after, I received everything I sent back through the post. Not only was the card, photos and letter I wrote returned, but also a card and gift that my parents sent to Kelly also that I had not known about.

I was heart-broken.

Meg had used the opportunity to return these things to me to respond to my letter also.

In it she stated "I'm really not happy with you or your family writing to Kelly. She is a child and you writing to her in the way that you do isn't fair on her. This really needs to stop now."

Meg went on to suggest that Kelly had come to terms with everything. I dreaded to think what Meg had told her had happened. The fact I was contacted shortly after I found out she wasn't mine by Kelly's school who said she'd told them she thought I was "ill or dying" showed that there had been issues. I counted that I was lucky to have seen her briefly a short time after that, by the chance meeting in the supermarket, to show her I was very much alive.

Meg continued, "This has been difficult for all of us to come to terms with, especially you and Kelly I know. The outcome was as much of a shock to me too." I doubted it really was a shock. Her reaction, at the mediation, said it all to me. She had actually laughed.

Meg, astoundingly, informed me "I pleaded with you at mediation but you made the decision to cut all contact and communication with Kelly. I'm sorry but you can't change that now, you need to stand by that decision." There was no pleading. Meg seemed more concerned with how she was going to cover childcare arrangements than what the effect of Kelly not seeing me would have had.

At the time I found out I was upset, confused and didn't know what to do for the best. I needed to come to terms with the knowledge I wasn't Kelly's biological father.

Meg again seemed to neglect to acknowledge the attempts I made at trying to resume contact following the court case. It seemed, to me, that Meg forgot her spiteful behaviour when I tried to reconcile things when she texted me saying "You'll never get near her again".

She went on further, "I don't want this to get nasty and I certainly don't want to fight with you anymore." So why reply at all then? Why not just throw the cards and photos and letters straight in the bin?

"You have been very vocal about not being Kelly's dad but you continue to sign everything as if you are. It's confusing for her. Please understand."

For me, it was never about *not* being Kelly's dad. It was about finding out about a lie and fighting against the injustice of a system that unfairly treated me once I found out. It was about Meg's attitude and reaction once I presented her with the proof. It was nothing to do with my actual relationship with Kelly. I loved, still love, that little girl.

She *was* my daughter and I *was* her dad and nothing would ever change that. It's true I couldn't change what happened and maybe I could have handled things better at the remediation and thereafter. But when the time came and I tried to reconcile, I was denied. Kelly was denied.

Being Kelly's father was a privilege. I had been gloriously happy being her dad. I just wasn't happy about the fact that it was all based on a lie, a deceit.

And it wasn't just the effect this had on me. My family, my mother in particular, were devastated by it.

I could never understand why a mother would prevent the only person that a child has known as their "dad" for seven and a half years from having contact with them. I believed Meg was deliberately spiteful – perhaps her only way of getting back at me for revealing the lie – by not allowing Kelly to see me.

Living with the loss, a kind of bereavement if you will was extremely difficult. It took two sets of counselling, the second over a period of several weeks, to get to a point where I could even talk about it to people. The pain and upset it caused me was unbearable and not something I'd wish on anyone. It drove me to think of doing something which is cowardly, shameful and not an answer and would only lead to more misery for those I love. It's embarrassing to talk about it, but I won't hide it as it's a part of understanding what I went through that's important.

I sat, one evening during the worst part of it all, with pills in my hand. The devastation, the loss, was too much to bear and I seriously thought about taking my own life.

I don't really know how it happened – whether I phoned her or she phoned me, but I ended up speaking to my Mum. It brings me to tears even now thinking about that moment. Without possibly knowing, or maybe she did know through some kind of connection a feeling which only a mother can have for their offspring, my Mum said all the right things to me. She was calm, delicate and soothing in her voice and I remember being reassured that things would be okay. Things would be alright.

I put the pills away and never went back to that dark place.

We're not ones for showing affection amongst our family very often but I remember seeing my mum shortly after and giving her a big hug and a kiss.

I wrote to Meg the following year, shortly after my Mum had a stroke – some of which the doctors said was brought on by stress of family situations, mine included, asking if Meg would allow my mother to see Kelly to help with her convalescence. I detailed that I needn't be involved in any way and gave her my parent's phone numbers so that it could be arranged.

I never got a response and my mother, to my knowledge, never did either and still hasn't seen Kelly.

Chapter Twenty-Two

After receiving the letter from Meg and the return of the photos, cards and letter, I had a call from Lois. I was clearly upset.

That evening, Lois came to my flat and declared she couldn't carry on with things as they were. She wasn't aware that I'd sent photographs and a letter, as well as the card, which she knew about, to Kelly. Although I hadn't lied to her about anything, I am sure she felt betrayed to some degree.

Lois said she was struggling to cope with it all and was considering going to the doctor to ask for anti-depressants. She didn't want to do that, and I wouldn't have wanted her to.

Things were strained between us. I'd already moved out of the flat we shared above her parent's house to another rented flat earlier in the year and had said back then that I thought we'd be "over" within six months.

When Lois arrived at the flat that day following work, she said that I had become obsessed with it all. Not just with the CSA battle but also with the loss of Kelly and that it was too much of a constant pain to be reminded of again and again.

The relationship between me and Lois was over. I was devastated. Once again, I lost something so precious to me.

Afterwards, I sat down and took a long hard look at myself. I got more counselling and packed things away. I packed away the photos and memories of Kelly and all the cards and letters I'd written.

When it came to putting away the photo of myself and Lois, I collapsed in the hallway. I felt a searing, emotional pain in my chest and cried out before I fell hard onto my knees. I sat, crying, shuddering, with the finality of it all. I felt lost, inconsolable and intolerably lonely.

I don't know how long I sat there for. But after I experienced that pain, that loneliness, I decided something had to change.

I put away all the communication with the CSA determining to let the Ombudsman just get on with it. Whatever would be, would be, I surmised.

The loss had changed me, changed my personality. I had realised that I had become so angry at what had happened to me, that it had started consuming me. It affected me, my behaviour, and my appearance - my weight in particular mostly through excessive drinking. My relationship with friends and, crucially, my relationship and life with my soul mate, Lois, was severely and terminally affected.

I'd previously been such a patient, calming influence on people and situations. Now I was just angry, impatient, uncaring. I used to be a fun guy to be around, the life and soul of the party. I stopped getting invited to parties, to events. I was depressing to be around.

It was no wonder Lois left me. Maybe she would have anyway, who knows, but it certainly didn't help us having to go through all of that.

And I didn't like what I'd become. I recognised I was driven to it by the extreme stresses of what the CSA put me through but was determined I wouldn't let it destroy me, or take anything further away from me.

I closed that chapter of my life and almost immediately felt better for having done so. No more obsessing. No more campaigning. It was done. I wouldn't dwell on what I lost in respect of Kelly. I would remember the happy times we had together.

Times such as when we were in the kitchen together baking cakes. Times when I shook the ketchup bottle and the lid came off covering me, Kelly and the kitchen in tomato sauce and a nervous moment passing between us before she smiled and started laughing, making me laugh.

I'd concentrate on that laughter, the joy, the absolute wonder and pleasure of being a part of, and influence upon, her life.

I would do nothing more than send a birthday card once a year to Kelly. And I would live in hope that maybe, one day, when she's old enough and wants to know what happened, that she'll contact me to ask why.

My life changed. I started losing weight and over the course of several months, got back to being "David" again. I was smiling, enjoying life and taking the bull by the horns.

I moved back "home" to Titchfield and found a place not far from where I used to live.

I got back to being what I was before the lie was found out and the situation thereafter all but destroyed me.

As old a cliché as it is, it's true: I found "myself" again.

Chapter Twenty-Three

It was coming up to Kelly's eleventh birthday when I realised Meg had moved house. Having passed by the house occasionally, and not having seen Meg's car parked outside the property for some time, it became apparent that she no longer lived there.

After dropping off a colleague who lived nearby, I saw Meg driving in her car in the opposite direction to that which I was travelling. I surmised that she probably *still* lived in the area.

A week or so later, I happened to pass by that way again. Meg's car was parked outside a house across the road from where she previously lived. No more than a hundred yards away!

* * *

On Kelly's eleventh birthday, Thursday 25th November 2010, having had no contact from her and not having seen her since the second chance encounter in the supermarket a year before when all I got to do was say "Hello Kelly.", I bought a card for her to wish her a "Happy Birthday" and to let her know I was still thinking of her every day.

I drove to where I previously had seen Meg's car parked outside the house. Meg's car wasn't there but a banner across the front door proclaimed that it was someone's birthday. That *had* to be the house.

I parked up a short distance away and walked towards the house, Kelly's card in my hand. I was shaking as I did so.

I took a chance that this was the correct house and quickly and quietly walked up the steps, ducking down beneath the kitchen window so I wouldn't be seen. It sounds like ridiculous behaviour and to a witness would have looked very suspicious I can imagine but the truth was that I just didn't want a confrontation with Meg or her new boyfriend; I just wanted to leave Kelly a card wishing her many happy returns on her eleventh birthday.

I was so nervous, I didn't even post the card through the letterbox! My heart was pounding. I was actually scared!

I left the card positioned on the doorstep so that it would be seen by anyone leaving or entering the house. I figured that with a party likely to be going on, someone arriving at the house would pick up the card and, hopefully, pass it to Kelly. I left as discreetly as I arrived and made my way back to the car and returned home.

* * *

On the morning of Saturday 27th November 2010, two days following the day I left a birthday card at Kelly's house, I went to the cinema with my friend Debbie.

My phone was on silent throughout the film and after we left the cinema, I checked it and found that, during the length of the film, I received several missed calls.

As I was checking the number, a mobile number which I didn't recognise, the phone rang again. It was the missed caller again. I very rarely answer the phone to an unknown caller as have previously been plagued by scammers, cold-callers and creditors or debt-collection agencies acting on those companies' behalf.

As this caller was somewhat persistent – they normally give up after a few failed attempts at getting through, I answered the phone and a gentleman on the end of the line advised me he was a police officer, calling himself "PC Hartman".

He claimed he was calling from Bracknell Police Station. He said that there had been a complaint in respect of the card I'd left on the doorstep for Kelly. The "police officer" made suggestions around "other letters" he'd seen that I'd sent earlier that year. The only letter I'd sent was asking Meg to let my Mum, following her stroke, to see Kelly to aid in her convalescence.

I found the fact that a policeman was phoning me to talk about a complaint they'd received quite unbelievable. Surely these things are handled face-to-face via a police officer or two attending my home or via a request for me to attend a police station to discuss the matter? To be contacted by phone just didn't seem right and I expressed this to the "officer".

"PC Hartman" said I was being given an "official warning". I told him, in no uncertain terms, that if he wanted me to believe he was a police officer that he should contact me via attendance at my home address and caution me appropriately. Until such time as that was to occur, I told him I had no interest in talking to him.

"PC Hartman" didn't take it too well when I told him that he should pursue the matter through a more official route rather than a phone call where anyone could be impersonating the police. I told him that I wasn't willing to accept anything he said and that he should take appropriate steps to enforce the message regarding the complaint against me by attending my home in person. I told him I was not prepared to discuss the matter any further by phone reminding him that he could be "anybody", and hung up the phone.

Later that day, around five hours after the call, I received a text message to my personal mobile phone at home. The phone I had with me at the cinema was my work-phone. I re-directed my personal mobile to my work phone for convenience so I'd only be carrying one phone around. I kept my personal phone on-going as it's a neat number that most of my friends, and some people who are not my friends any longer, know and contact me via.

The text message read:

David Gates, please read. My name is PC 4261 Hartman from Bracknell Police Station. Thames Valley Police non-emergency number is xxxxxxxxxx if you wish to confirm who I am. A letter has been sent to [my address] explaining what I tried to tell you on the phone. What i [sic] told you over the phone IS an official harassment warning, and can be given in any form which is appropriate. Should it be reported that you have attended Meg's home address, or attempted to make contact with her or Kelly, then you WILL be arrested. If you have any questions, feel free to call if you are wiling [sic] to have a conversation about the matter. PC Hartman.

I was astonished. Either this was a wind-up, someone pretending to be the police, or the police had started sending warnings by text! Surely, before I am warned in this manner I should be officially cautioned? It seemed so bizarre that I decided to ignore it.

Several days later I received a letter which also didn't quite look genuine. It looked like it had been photocopied. Something about it, the way it was handwritten on the envelope, just didn't gel.

I took the letter into a local police station and asked the officer there if he could confirm if it was genuine. He took it into the office and returned a few minutes later stating just "Yes." Nothing more than that. All he said was "Yes".

I'm still not one-hundred per-cent convinced as to the genuineness or legality or the phone call, text and letter.

That said, I decided not to take the risk that it was falsified. It's too much of a risk for me, especially given some aspects of my job where I can find myself working with children from time to time, to push the issue. If I was arrested for harassment, or had my name tarnished in some way associated with an approach toward a minor for example, despite it being just the innocent sending of a birthday card, it could result in my losing my job or having restrictions placed upon me. Who knows what could happen. In a worst case scenario, I could even be imprisoned.

Stalking and harassment are very serious issues indeed. For the victim it can be a genuinely scary experience and one which no-one should have to go through.

Whether the complaint made by Meg is genuine or not doesn't really matter. I don't consider that I am a stalker, nor do I consider that the sending of a single card once a year is harassment.

But I had to make a decision on how to continue. Erring on the side of caution, and despite not being confident this wasn't a friend of Meg's abusing their position, I decided to step back and not rattle this particular cage.

I took a different approach for Kelly's subsequent birthdays. For each of Kelly's next birthdays, I took to buying a card for her and writing a message inside it for her. I dated the back of the envelope and placed the card in a box of keepsakes and memories I have of her.

Should the time come when I see her again, I can give her the cards and explain why it was I wasn't able to send or give them to her.

I think it's important for her, should she wish, to know that I never forgot her.

And never would.

Chapter Twenty-Four

In December 2010, nearly eighteen months after I'd instructed the Parliamentary Ombudsman to review the CSA and ICE handling of my case, they wrote to me sending me a draft report of their findings.

In short, the Ombudsman upheld my complaint. They also made recommendations to the CSA to reconsider all the maintenance payments that I made and to exercise their discretion to arrive at a proper decision on any reimbursement due to me. It was determined that should they decide to refund me any money, they should pay me interest on that money from 25th June 2008.

They also recommended that the Agency provide me with an apology for the way in which they handled my case and a £300 consolatory payment to recognise the impact of their maladministration. The Ombudsman also recommended the ICE provide me with an apology for the way in which they handled my case.

Unfortunately, due to Section 11 of the Parliamentary Commissioner Act 1967, I am prohibited from disclosing any part of the report.

But I felt wholly vindicated. The CSA had put me through hell and were being asked to reconsider their reasons for not refunding me the maintenance in full. They either had to refund me, something I doubted they'd do, or provide very clear reasons as to why they were not refunding me.

*   *   *

On 11th January 2011, I still hadn't heard anything from the ICE or CSA. I wrote an email to the Ombudsman detailing this and they advised they had received a letter from the CSA which should have been forwarded to me.

The letter from the CSA contained the apology "for the poor level of service you have received from the Agency. It is clear that we have not dealt with your case in an appropriate manner."

The letter went on to state that when I first disputed my parentage, in August 2007, "the Agency should have advised you of the appropriate action to take in order for you to resolve your dispute immediately. If we had provided you with accurate information at the outset, you would have been able to gain a declaration of non-parentage from the courts sooner and subsequently this would have resulted in an earlier closure of your case. It is unacceptable that our procedures were not fully explained to you and it is clear we caused you delay."

They went on to tell me it was "clear that we did not give you the right advice about the payment you have made through both the Agency and direct to the parent with care.

Our guidance states that if a non-resident parent is later found not to be the parent of the child payments should be refunded. When your case was closed we refunded to you the payments you have made through the Agency and advised you any payments made direct to the parent with care would not be refunded. As our guidance does not differentiate between payments made through the Agency and those made direct to the parent with care we should have considered and refunded the payments you made in that way."

I had to turn over the page to read the next part.

"We have decided that you should receive a refund for the payments you made directly to the parent with care to the sum of £14745.88".

"You will also receive an additional payment of £1043.42 as interest in recognition of the loss of use of these monies since 25 June 2008". The letter continued.

Finally, the letter noted I'd get the £300 consolatory payment and the full amount would be paid within ten working days. It actually appeared in my bank within three.

The letter ended with "Whilst these payments are not large amounts they are tangible recognition of the maladministration that has occurred on your case. There is no right of appeal against this decision but if you have further evidence we will be happy to reconsider the decision. Please accept my sincere apologies for the errors that have been made on your case, the poor quality of client service and the inconvenience this has caused you."

I broke down. I physically fell from my seat onto the floor and lay there crying. I must have cried solidly for about ten or fifteen minutes. I couldn't speak. I could barely breathe.

I eventually managed to phone my Mum and Dad and tell them about it. I then phoned my mate Debbie to let her know the news.

It was all finally over. I felt a weight was lifted and that justice had finally been done. All the pain I'd been through, the stress, the loss of Kelly, losing Lois and my own well-being, was finally recognised.

Kelly lost her Dad and the family she'd had in the shape of cousins, aunties and uncles and grandparents as a result of all of this.

I wonder if it was all worth it. To uncover a lie. To reveal the truth. There may have been things that, on reflection, I could have done differently. But ultimately I live with what I did because I feel I did the right thing.

The money would come in useful but I'd lost something that was worth much, much more which no amount of money could account for.

I'd lost my daughter, Kelly, and I'd lost my soul-mate, Lois.

Chapter Twenty-Five

It's funny how little things remind me of her. The following may seem somewhat random, but its things like these that keep her in my memory.

Like whenever I use the toilet at my mate Greg's house. I remember one sunny day when we stopped off there as I needed to pick something up. Kelly needed to use the loo just before we left and being nervous about being in a strange house and, as I was at the front door with Greg, needed reassurance I wouldn't leave without her, she went to the toilet at the top of the stairs and left the door open so she could still see me and be sure I hadn't left her.

Now, some times when I use that same toilet, it reminds me of what happened that day.

Another happy memory I have is me, Kelly and Lois's dog Brian, taking a walk along the beach at Rockley Park, near Poole in Dorset. We walked along the pier and the beach, Kelly finding all manner of stones and shells she wanted to bring home to give to Lois.

When Kelly was just a baby, either pram-bound or car-seat bound as still unable to walk, I would take her to the working farm at Manor Farm and Country Park near Hedge End in Hampshire. There she could see, probably for the first time, pigs, sheep, cattle, chickens, ducks and geese.

As we were moving down the path to the pond to feed the ducks, something Kelly could do from the buggy, curious geese came up to Kelly and either sniffed or nipped at her toes causing her to cry and causing me to have to shoo them away.

One of Kelly's favourite songs was by Blondie. One Way or Another was one she sang along to, particularly when it got to the lyric, "I'm gonna get ya', get ya', get ya', get ya'"

But one of my most precious memories is that of when we went to Victoria Park, which leads down to Southampton water.

Kelly was not long at school and we walked along the nature path in the woods that would lead us down to the sea. As we walked through the woods, we came across a raised wooden pathway that enabled you to walk across the ponds and marshy environment.

It was quiet, the sound of traffic dulled into submission by the foliage and trees and only the sound of songbirds, likely warning of the invaders to their territories, could be heard.

Then, suddenly, a loud cracking sound from across the water which sat between the "bridges" we were on and the steep bank that went up several tens of feet opposite was heard. I held Kelly close to me and knelt down, hugging her close and pointing across the water to what I'd seen and urging her not to make any sound by placing my finger to my mouth.

Three deer stood upon the bank, about four feet higher up than we were, above the water line. A moment passed and I caught Kelly smiling, the wondrous sight of these beautiful animals in front of us.

Almost as soon as we'd seen them, they broke their stance and ran up the bank and deeper into the woods. Within seconds, they were gone from view.

It had been a magical moment that Kelly and I shared. Wondrous and almost dream-like in its perfection.

Even now, when I revisit the same spot, I remember that moment and what we shared that no-one else did.

Being Kelly's Dad was an absolute privilege. One of the most joyous times of my life. And I would like to think hers too. We shared a lot of things together. And a love that was unconditional in every sense. Not a day goes by when I don't think of her.

More than words could ever describe, I miss her.

Chapter Twenty-Six

<u>I Miss You</u>

I miss the sound of your laugh,
I miss you splashing in the bath,
I miss your gorgeous smile,
I miss you, all the while.

I miss you being my cheeky monkey,
I miss you dancing to something funky,
I miss you more and more each day,
I miss you more than words can say.

I miss the time we used to have together,
I miss us going out in all sorts of weather,
I miss buying you presents and taking you places,
I miss you making funny faces.

I miss your questions about everything,
I miss the sound of hearing you sing,
I miss you so much; it hurts in my belly,
I miss you so much, my darling Kelly.

Appendix One

The History of the CSA

In the late 1980's, the increasing cost on the Treasury of benefits paid to lone parent families was brought to the attention of the then Prime Minister Margaret Thatcher by an MP.

This proved to be the beginnings of a scheme that started out with the best of intentions, but very quickly became little more than a mechanism for reimbursing the Treasury and in so doing creating financial hardship for thousands of families.

Government had two stated aims - to reduce child poverty and to make non-resident parents responsible for the financial upkeep of their children, thereby relieving the taxpayer of that burden. Ministers initially supported the proposed legislation and its approach. However, despite being advised against doing so, the focus of the child support scheme was on recovering monies for the Treasury rather than on the welfare of the child and the legislation was written to reflect this. Parents with care were to see no financial gain in co-operating with the scheme and non-resident parents objected because the legislation was made in retrospect, which overturned previous divorce settlements. Such settlements were disregarded and the non-resident parent was made to pay all over again.

The Child Support Act 1991 was passed to give the necessary powers for a system to collect child support. Within 2 years of the Child Support Act being passed, the CHILD SUPPORT AGENCY was born and became the vehicle by which this Act was to be executed. The system they introduced was extremely complex and, as it turned out, directly conflicted with the aim to reduce child poverty. The agency was manned by inexperienced staff using an IT system that was hopelessly inadequate for the workload placed upon it.

Dogged by error and conflicting aims, the agency was a failure, with inefficient administration and problems caused by the IT system being evident from the outset. What MPs and Ministers had feared had come to pass.

Ill trained staff was subjected to increasing pressure to meet unrealistic targets, and as the volume of work increased, it led to a high absence rate and low morale. Before long, the agency received an instruction to "maximise the maintenance yield". Staff reacted to this by targeting those non-resident parents who were more likely to pay maintenance than those who would require time and resources to pursue. And so the 'brown envelope' culture was formed. The parent with care, who had previously struggled to secure maintenance and had turned to the CSA as their saviour to retrieve money from the non-resident parent, soon realised this was not going to happen. Non-resident parents who had private arrangements in place were told these arrangements were no longer valid and payments were to commence as instructed by the formula laid down in law. The system quickly became the target of fierce opposition and parents took to the streets in protest. Finally, Government began to realise the truth of the concerns previously raised by Ministers.

A New Beginning:

Public resistance and high levels of criticism lead to the new Labour Government introducing a simplified system in March 2003 (CS2). This system was to use a new, simplified formula to calculate the liability for maintenance based on percentages and this, together with a new £450 million computer system, was meant to be the saving of the CSA. The vision was never realised. The reality was that parents with care with errant ex partners continued to struggle to secure regular maintenance, despite the CSA's new campaign to target non-paying parents. Non-resident parents who had no intention of paying up were, once again, able to slip easily through the net.

A New, New Beginning:

After 13 years of more errors, criticism, and millions of pounds of taxpayer's money wasted, Sir David Henshaw was asked by the Secretary of State for Work and Pensions to produce a redesigned child support system. A damning report, written by Sir David in July 2006, recommended the Child Support Agency as it stood should cease to exist and a 'radical' new system put in place. The report focused on the welfare of the child and to reduce child poverty, which the CS Act had painfully failed to achieve. Government took on board these recommendations and responded with their proposal for the Child Maintenance and Enforcement Commission (CMEC). This commission will work at 'arm's length' from the Government and will primarily encourage parents to make their own arrangements for child support.

Whilst there are some measures within the proposals for CMEC to be welcomed, overall they amount to nothing more than a re-hash of the old system, despite the 'radical new approach hyped by the Secretary of State for Work and Pensions in his announcement. Some of the new powers of enforcement to be given to the commission will have far-reaching effects.

NACSA (National Association for Child Support Action) is a leading organisation within the UK that specialise in giving advice, providing information and supporting non-resident parents when injustices occur.

NACSA lobby against the unfair practices of the CSA and since their creation in 1993, have helped thousands of families obtain justice. Their aim is to provide affordable help to those suffering the inaccuracies and heavy-handed administration of the Child Support Act.

Many of NACSA's members have given their views on some of these proposals and NACSA does not believe that CMEC will address the concerns and problems voiced by them. Today's changing family structures demand a more pragmatic approach to child support and NACSA will continue to lobby government and ministers in an effort to get a fair and acceptable system of child support established.

The Key elements of CMEC include:

• Removing the compulsory element for parents with care claiming a prescribed benefit to use CSA services for child support arrangements. Parents with care will be free to make private arrangements with the non-resident parent and will no longer suffer a reduction in benefit.

• Overseeing an administration process in which parents can register their own private arrangements for child support.

• Providing extensive information, guidance and support to parents to fully inform them of the options available to them.

• Increasing the maintenance disregard. Currently parents with care (on the new rules system) receive the first £10 of any maintenance paid. Legislation will extend these rules to encompass old rules PWCs to benefit from the £10 disregard. By 2011 this disregard is proposed to be substantially increased.

• CMEC will operate on the percentage based scheme as seen in CS2 rules but income of the NRP will be taken from the latest available tax information.

• Child maintenance will be calculated on the gross income of the NRP.

• Percentage rates will be set at 12% for one child 16% for two children and 19% for three or more children.

• Increasing the capping of income from £2000 pw to £3000 pw

- One year fixed term payment schedules will be imposed, with variations to maintenance payable allowed only if a minimum 25% change of income is reported.

- Increasing current flat rate amounts from £5 pw to £7 pw

- Using Deduction from Earnings Orders as a first method of collecting maintenance payments. This will allow CMEC to take the maintenance directly from the wages of the non-resident parent.

- Removing the need to take non-resident parents to court before pursuing a debt. Currently a liability order has to be granted by the courts before recovery action can be taken. CMEC will introduce an administrative process to replace the court based liability order process.

- Extend avenues available to secure information on non-resident parents.

- Outsource debt collection to Debt Collection Agencies who will have extended powers of entry.

Other proposals under consideration are:

- Introduce powers to confiscate passports, driving licences, introduce curfews, and tagging of non-paying non-resident parents.

- Introduce a "name and shame" program, making public the details of non-resident parents who have failed to pay maintenance. Further consultation is in place for this particular proposal.

- Introduce a charging regime for the use of CMEC services.

- Shared care arrangements to remain as that in CS2, but with the provision to allow an interim decision on presumed shared care arrangements until the matter has been confirmed.

- Consideration and further consultation is being given to make joint birth registration compulsory.

These proposals are currently working their way through the parliamentary process, with an expected date of introduction as 2011-2013. Some of the proposals are not yet defined; others may be altered as they work through parliamentary debate. If you have any concerns about the CMEC proposals now is the time to raise them. It is imperative that you write to your MP to express your views before the proposals become law.

NACSA gave evidence to the Dept. Works and Pensions Select Committee in January 2007 in which they expressed their concerns over some of the CMEC proposals. They also provided a written submission to the consultation process. You can read their submission and get help from NACSA at www.nacsa.co.uk

Appendix Two

Letter to the Department of Work and Pensions

Re: David Gates – v – Department for Work and Pensions

Thank you for your letter of 23 April 2008.

We note that you propose to make a refund to our client in respect of payments made by him through the Child Support Agency of £2,137.28.

We are instructed that on 22 April 2008 and 28 April 2008 our client spoke by telephone with Mr. Adam West at your office. On both occasions Mr West informed our client that our client would receive not only repayment of the sum referred to above in respect of the payments made through the CSA but also all of the monies paid by him directly to the parent with care pursuant to the special dispensation that the CSA can apply in such cases. This totals £22,865.88. We enclose a breakdown of the funds paid during the period 16 May 2001 to 3 July 2007 directly to the parent with care from our client which totaled £19,265.88. The balance of £3,600 relates to the earlier period of April 2000 to April 2001.

In the second telephone conversation with Mr Adam West of 28 April 2008, our client queried whether the CSA would in fact refund him the full monies due in view of your letter of 23 April 2008 in which you have indicated that he would only be paid the sum of £2,137.28. Mr West informed our client that it had been too late to stop the letter going out but that he had already raised this with your policy team.

On 29 April 2008 our client was informed by telephone by Mr. West that payment would only be made to him in accordance with the letter which you had sent and that he would not be refunded the full sum in maintenance which he had paid directly to the parent with care. Naturally our client is most confused and angry at being told initially that he would be paid the full sum due and subsequently being told now that this payment was not forthcoming.

It is clearly quite unacceptable for your department to confirm agreement to a payment being made and then to retract this without any good reason. Our client paid the monies to the parent with care in good faith believing him to be the father of the child and it is therefore only right that he should be fully compensated now that the correct position with regard to paternity has been established.

Our client also claims the legal costs and expenses in respect of establishing that he is not the father of the child including the DNA testing.

We note that in your letter you state that the DNA testing was instigated by our client and not at the request of the agency. This is not correct. Our client initially arranged private DNA testing of himself and the child without the involvement of the mother which confirmed that he was not the father. Those test results were presented to both the CSA and the mother. The CSA were not willing to accept the test results without full testing of all three parties. It was therefore at the request of the CSA that further testing was undergone to establish paternity. Our client is not claiming a refund in respect of the initial DNA tests which he undertook privately but he is seeking repayment of the DNA tests which were subsequently undertaken and involved the parent with care, the child and himself. Regrettably the mother was not willing to cooperate with testing and it was for this reason that a Court application was made pursuant to the Family Law Act 1986 for a declaration of non-parentage. With respect we refer you to your department's letter of 5 October 2007, a further copy of which we enclose for ease of reference in which you confirmed that our client "is doing the right thing by applying to the Court for a declaration of non-paternity".

We also refer you to your website in which again it is confirmed that reimbursement will be made to the father of the cost of DNA tests in these circumstances.

We note that you state that the agency was not a party to the application on paternity and is therefore not prepared to pay legal costs associated with the application. We would respectfully refer you to our letter of 21 September 2007 in which we invited your department to intervene in the proceedings; you declined that invitation in your letter of 5 October 2007. The declaration of non-parentage which was made by the Court on 3 March 2008 confirms that our client is not the father of the child concerned and since this declaration binds not only the parties of the case but anyone else to whom this is relevant including the CSA, we would respectfully suggest that the CSA should reimburse our client for the legal costs incurred.

In all the circumstances we would therefore invite you to reimburse our client in full for all maintenance payments made by him whether directly to the parent with care or through the agency and for the costs of the Court proceedings and DNA testing totaling £29,154.49.

In the event that payment is not made to our client with 14 days of the date of this letter of the full sum due further Court proceedings will be taken without notice to you and a claim for costs made in this respect.

Appendix Three

Letter to the Independent Case Examiner

The specifics of my complaint in response to the numbered sections of your report are as follows:

2. The investigation has taken a year to complete. Yet, the report doesn't refer to a number of items in my original complaint and looks to have been cobbled together in a matter of days. I was also informed, at the start, that the case would be reviewed and the expectation was it would take six months to complete. The delay incurred by the CSA in providing information in relation to you being able to start the case is quoted as being seven weeks. This is incorrect. The delay was substantially longer than seven weeks. On 29th November 2008, it had already been a month and I wrote to you regarding this and citing this as further evidence of the CSA's maladministration. I wrote to you again on 18th December 2008 as by then you STILL had not received the information from the CSA, despite escalating the issue within the CSA. I wrote AGAIN on 23rd January 2009 as by this time you STILL had not received the information required to start the investigation. That is three months. Not seven weeks.

3. A. I was advised by the CSA to take the PWC to court. Given that the CSA advised me of this as being the correct action; it is not unreasonable to expect the CSA to cover these costs.

3. B. On 6th October, I received a letter from the CSA detailing: "Your client is doing the right thing by applying to the court for a declaration of non-paternity" – therefore, sanctioning that I **have** to go to court to prove my innocence. The letter goes on to state "In cases where a calculation has been made and the NRP (Non-Resident Parent) has accepted parentage,… if he then disputes parentage this is treated as a request for revision by the Agency." I contend that the Agency carried out NO such revision. The letter goes on to state that

"the NRP must apply to the court...." As the Agency is INSTRUCTING me to go to court, it is my contention that the CSA should bear the ultimate costs of that should I win my case (which I did!)

3. C. I have a physical audio recording from April 2008 whereby Mr. Adam West admits that he told me I would be getting the money I paid to the CSA **and** the PWC back. He confirmed I would be getting it all back. This occurred on at least TWO occasions. He even quoted me a figure of "around £13,000" and there was conversation around the fact that he had made recommendations to the policy unit for me to be refunded as the situation was "not satisfactory". He even took my bank details to expedite the refund!
From my original complaint:
Mr. West most DEFINITELY told me, on at least two occasions, that I would be reimbursed for the payments made directly to the PWC. I taped the conversation and can provide it as evidence if required. Mr West specifically said, on 28th April 2008, in response to my referencing our conversation the Tuesday before (22nd April 2008), in which I queried:
- Mr. D. E. Gates: "And you said that I would be getting back all of the money that I'd previously paid directly to Miss Griffin?"
- Mr. West: "Yes."

Even after consulting the policy team, Mr. West STILL maintained I would be getting all of my money paid directly to Miss Griffin back.

3. D. There were two DOE's (Deduction of Earnings Orders) issued against me. They were incorrectly submitted:
- The order does not detail the type of work I do.
- The order does not detail my works number.
- The order does not detail the amount or amounts to be taken and the dates of any change to these amounts in the next 52 weeks
- The order does not detail my protected earnings rate.

3. E. The evidence I have supplied CLEARLY details the delays, maladministration, poor service, direct incompetence (Mr. Adam

West, on the tape recording, even says "That was just my incompetence"). I believe that some significant form of financial redress for maladministration should be forthcoming due to the sustained and ongoing incompetence and delays I've had to suffer at the CSA's hands. In the CSA's own words, I should receive a payment **"if our action or lack of action caused: serious inconvenience as a result of repeated mistakes."** Also, from the DWP website: the following justifications for maladministration, are clear: **"neglect, inattention, delay, incompetence, ineptitude"** Mr. West directly admitted his incompetence in misreading the legislation. And finally, from the Ombudsman website: **"Maladministration generally means poor administration or the wrong application of rules"**. The previously supplied "diary" details clearly the poor administration and application of rules.

4. You mention you have examined the information provided by myself and the Agency yet you still come to the conclusion not to uphold my complaints. I fail to see how this is possible given the significant amount of information and evidence I have submitted. It is my belief that you have simply chosen not to refer to my evidence in favour of the CSA.

5. As previously detailed, the delay was significantly longer than seven weeks. In fact, it was nearly TWICE as long as this.

6. The agency clearly does not take your recommendations seriously. Otherwise, why would it take the agency three months to provide the information you requested from them, or even act upon your requests?

7. A. Given that I am not in the legal profession, I was forced to engage with a solicitor who knew the process in respect of obtaining a declaration of non-parentage as my initial case, where I attempted to place the request to the court under my own knowledge, was found to be incorrectly submitted and was very nearly dismissed. As the CSA would not accept anything but the formal and correct declaration, and would not assist me either, it was imperative that the process be completed accurately. The procedure for obtaining a declaration of non-parentage is very complicated and has to be

undertaken in a very specific way. Neil Goldman from the CSA, in August 2007, informed me I would be repaid all associated costs with obtaining the declaration. On 6th October, I received a letter from the CSA detailing: "Your client is doing the right thing by applying to the court for a declaration of non-paternity" – therefore, sanctioning that I **have** to go to court to prove my innocence. As the Agency is INSTRUCTING me to go to court, it is my contention that the CSA should bear the ultimate costs of that should I win my case (which I did!). Further to this, and by your own admission, "professional fees may only be considered where maladministration has occurred and the engagement of professional help was justified in the pursuit of a child maintenance issue." As this was in pursuit of a child maintenance issue (I either continued paying child maintenance for a child I knew not to be mine, or I went to court), and you concur that the agency has been maladministrative in its dealings with me, it should refund appropriately.

8. Whilst this is not relevant in my particular case, because there was no initial doubt regarding paternity (this came later), it is simply wrong that the NRP has to prove he's not the father rather than the PWC prove that he is.

9. I produced evidence to the CSA that cast doubt on my parentage [of Kelly]. The CSA refused to assist me and actively obstructed me in getting the case reviewed. The CSA refused to provide me with a list of DNA test centres, despite several requests.

10. Your comments in relation to your "serious concerns about the manner in which this test was carried out at your instigation" are misplaced and inappropriate. It is not the ICE's place to comment on anything outside of the direct dealings I had with the CSA and I believe this personal viewpoint is creating an unfair bias against me. For your information, in respect of my taking the DNA test, I did NOTHING WRONG. I did not do ANYTHING that was illegal. Your comments and any view in relation to this matter should be struck from the report and disregarded as they are entirely inappropriate. It is not the ICE's job to judge events outside of the complaint. I cite this as specific maladministration in your investigation.

11. There appears to be an error when you state that I detailed "the officer you had spoken to on 14 August 2007 had advised that the costs would not be refunded". I made no such assertion.

12. I refer you to my response detailed in 7. A. Further to this, I received a letter from the Independent Case Examiner that said that my complaint related to "Child Support Legislation." My complaint clearly didn't relate to this and I again wrote to the Independent Case Examiner detailing dozens of examples of maladministration.

13. This is incorrect, in every respect. On 17th September 2007, I wrote to the agency, John Herbert specifically, asking him to send me every piece of information the CSA have on file relative to me and regarding my case. I also ask him to send me a full account breakdown of all monies paid to the CSA from myself. I detail that I've had to ask for this no less than **four times** previously without getting a response that fulfilled the requests.
In regard to that which Miss Griffin "confirms", it should be noted that the judge made NO RECOMMENDATION that Miss Griffin should continue with Agency action. No mention of the agency was made at any time at the hearing on 13th September. The hearing was to advise on evidence to be submitted and a further hearing to be conducted on 23rd November 2007. I there had been any recommendation of this nature, it would be on the court orders, of which I have copies, and it is not.

14. I don't have any "case synopsis" as detailed. The only things I received around this time were two Detachment of Earnings orders which, I understand, were mysteriously rushed through.

15. There seems to be a huge gap in everything that occurred during October, November and December of 2007 which details the maladministration I frequently referred to. It is not referenced in any way. I cite this as your refusal to acknowledge some of my evidence.

16. By telling me that I had to go to court to obtain the declaration of non-parentage, and by informing me that "all costs associated with obtaining the DNA test" and the declaration of non-parentage would

be refunded, the CSA are complicit in these costs being incurred. At the very least, the court costs should be refunded.

B. 17. By your own admission, "professional fees may only be considered where maladministration has occurred and the engagement of professional help was justified in the pursuit of a child maintenance issue." As this was in pursuit of a child maintenance issue (I either continued paying child maintenance for a child I knew not to be mine, or I went to court), the agency should refund appropriately. I have already cited the numerous instances of maladministration in my diary and original complaint.

18. Mr. West most DEFINITELY told me, on at least two occasions, that I would be reimbursed for the payments made directly to the PWC. I taped the conversation and can provide it as evidence if required. Mr West specifically said, on 28th April 2008, in response to my referencing our conversation the Tuesday before (22nd April 2008), in which I queried:
- Mr. D. E. Gates: "And you said that I would be getting back all of the money that I'd previously paid directly to Miss Griffin?"
- Mr. West: "Yes."

These comments are further confirmed in the letter from my solicitor that you referred to in No. 19.

Even after consulting the policy team, Mr. West STILL maintained I would be getting all of my money paid directly to Miss Griffin back. Why is it that I'm told one thing several times by one department and another by the solicitor? There seems to be no reason for Mr. West's recommendations to have been dismissed.

19. This is the first item which is accurate in your report.

I found it astounding that it was nineteen points into their report until I found something I agreed with or that was wholly accurate. Absolutely astounding.

20. As per 18 above, the Agency HAD CONFIRMED I would be REFUNDED ALL PAYMENTS PAID DIRECT to Miss Griffin. The officer, on 22nd April, did not say "may". He said "would". I have it on audio recording:
- Mr. D. E. Gates: "And you said that I would be getting back all of the money that I'd previously paid directly to Miss Griffin?"
- Mr. West: "Yes."

You also go on to state the agency said "Miss Griffin did not confirm, when contacted, that the direct payments were in lieu of child maintenance". This is INCORRECT. Miss Griffin confirmed that the payments I made directly to her **were** in lieu of child support maintenance. The CSA detail she has confirmed this in the letter I received from the CSA on 21st January 2008.

21. I never suggested it was Agency maladministration that led me to challenge paternity. However, once I did challenge it, the Agency was deliberately obstructive and misleading and I have already cited numerous examples of maladministration in relation to my progression of obtaining the declaration of non-parentage.

22. I only engaged with a solicitor due to the complicated nature of the court case procedures and in response to your officer informing me that "all costs associated with the obtaining of the declaration of non-parentage" would be refunded.

23. Given that you have ignored numerous examples of maladministration and evidence provided that CLEARLY demonstrate the "**action or lack of action [that] caused: serious inconvenience as a result of repeated mistakes**" and "**neglect, inattention, delay, incompetence, ineptitude**", I am aghast and bewildered that you should come to such a conclusion to not uphold my complaint and I would again suggest that you are biased towards the CSA – this is further amplified by the personal comments you made in respect to how I discovered I was not the father initially.

C. 24. No comment.

25. Please note that the sum of £2,137.28 was the monies I paid directly to the agency. At all times, the agency was made aware of the payments, in lieu of child maintenance, I made directly to the PWC. Miss Griffin had confirmed this – if she had not, the arrears would have been significantly higher.

26. Correct.

27. Correct.

28. Correct.

29. I am happy to dissolve the requirement of the agency to refund any payments made direct to the PWC PRIOR to July 2002.

30. This is probably the most ridiculous statement you have made. "I found no evidence that you raised a paternity dispute". What the hell are the letters I have from the agency that detail my dispute and that you referred to earlier in this very report then?? The CSA acknowledged my paternity dispute in September 2007!! I find it absolutely absurd that you then go on to say the CSA had "no grounds" to refund the monies it took from me under the DOE order. Even without maladministration, the Agency was required to refund all payments once I proved I was not the father.
You also state that I "waited five years before challenging that acceptance." I did not "wait" as you put it. I simply discovered that the child in question was not mine after this time and it was at this discovery I raised the paternity dispute with the agency. I had no cause prior to this to dispute the child was not mine.
The sums I have received **are proper** and I was **entitled** to receive them. Your suggestion that these payments were not proper is not correct. You also agree that "The Agency can in certain situations refund payments of maintenance where an alleged non-resident parent is proved not to be the parent following a paternity dispute". I proved I was not the parent, so the agency should refund the payments of maintenance made in line with this policy.
I feel that your personal view is causing bias in respect of this item and again cite this as maladministration. It is clear you have not understood the facts of this.

D. 31. At no time did the agency allow me to come to an arrangement regarding maintenance. If you look at the timeline for the communications and even the cheque I sent in September, you can quite clearly see that the DOE order was rushed through. I have it on advisement that the normal time to process a DOE is considerably longer than that which the agency on this occasion took. Further to this, the DOE was incorrect in its submission as detailed previously:
- The order does not detail the type of work I do.
- The order does not detail my works number.
- The order does not detail the amount or amounts to be taken and the dates of any change to these amounts in the next 52 weeks
- The order does not detail my protected earnings rate.

The fact I was sent TWO DOE's with DIFFERING DATES AND AMOUNTS, is also an example of the CSA's maladministration. This is something you seemed to have ignored also.

32. I was NEVER advised of a possible DOE order being made against me. The first I knew about it was when my employer informed me it had been received. I believe this rushing through of the DOE was against agency procedure and that someone at the CSA was on a vendetta against me and pushed it through to assist Miss Griffin and to cause me un-necessary hardship. At NO TIME before this order was completed, was I given an opportunity at the place that issues such orders, to appeal. The order was put in place without my being able to intervene or address the issue during the proceedings – this strikes me as severely unfair as I should, if having an order made against me, be able to represent myself like any other defendant would have, to present my case against said order. The order detailed £1,005.06 to be taken on 03/10/07, £671.40 on 03/11/07 and £558.82 monthly from 03/12/07. This put me under extreme hardship as this was more than 50% of my take-home salary!! Also, given the agency's statement that my arrears were nil, I struggle to find where they got these figures from.

As previously detailed from the court case to which you refer, it should be noted that the judge made NO RECOMMENDATION that

Miss Griffin should continue with Agency action. No mention of the agency was made at any time at the hearing on 13th September. The hearing was to advise on evidence to be submitted and a further hearing to be conducted on 23rd November 2007. No reference was made to a deduction of earnings order during the hearing also.

I should like to ask where you are obtaining this information from as to what occurred at a court case at which the CSA or ICE was not present. Again, I feel there is a mis-information going on here I believe it is possible the CSA records detail that Miss Griffin has advised of these things – but I can categorically state that this is NOT the case. If it had been, it would have been on the court orders of which I have copies of. It is not. Your report is not clear on where this "evidence" comes from and as there is no basis for it in fact; reference to it should be struck from the report.

33. As previously detailed, it is curious to note that the DOE order is processed within a matter of just two and a half weeks. This is in spite of the fact that a cheque for payment was sent around 4th September. Normal DOE's take considerably longer to process. I would question as to how mine was miraculously processed in days when anything else the CSA does takes weeks or months. There's also the question of a person from the CSA contacting my employer directly to "chase up" the DOE. My employer stated that this was "most unusual" behaviour from the CSA.

34. I wrote, enclosing the completed and appropriate forms, to the Central Appeals Unit to appeal against the DOE. Again, for some reason, this letter was not officially received by the Agency until 23rd October 2007. **I do not believe it took the Post Office TWO WEEKS to deliver my letter!!** The Tribunals Service says it's unable to investigate or comment on the DOE. It says that the appeal must be lodged with the decision making agency before they can be sent to the Tribunals Service – I ALREADY DID THAT!! The CSA tells me my APPEAL is outside of the jurisdiction of the Central Appeals Unit and the Tribunal Service. It tells me I should write to my magistrates to appeal the order. I cite this as MIS-INFORMING me of the procedure as the TRIBUNALS SERVICE on 26th October 2007 informed me that I had to contact the agency first!! Again, MORE maladministration and delay.

35. This is incorrect. Miss Griffin did not request the order be stopped. Jonathan Weed's investigations led to the DOE being stopped. It would appear, based on this that the CSA was able to withdraw the DOE without the need for me to have to be referred to the magistrates' court. I cite this as further examples of incompetence and misdirection and maladministration.

36. If there is no provision within the procedures, how is it that Jonathan Weed was able to get the DOE withdrawn? Clearly, there ARE provisions. The very fact that the DOE was full of mistakes therefore making it incorrectly placed as cited in D.31. above, is a clear example of maladministration and I contest your decision not to uphold this element of my complaint.

E. 37. I have detailed in my diary the additional stress the agency caused. The errors and incompetence and maladministration I have referred to ably demonstrate this and I should, as your comment states, be compensated for it. I have also provided witness testimony from my fiancée's doctor that corroborates the stress she experienced as a direct result of the agency's behaviour.

38. The agency continually failed to provide a service I was entitled to. The result was maladministration on a grand scale.

39. Whilst I did not detail any maladministration prior to my paternity dispute, I have detailed considerable maladministration that occurred thereafter. You even agree that the agency did not respond to my enquiries. Therefore, you are agreeing that maladministration has occurred and you should uphold this aspect of my complaint.

40. You state that the agency replied to my communication of 31st July 2007 on 5th September: "This was two weeks outside of its charter standard". Therefore, you agree with me that there was delay and I cite this as further evidence of maladministration. You should therefore uphold this element of my complaint.

41. You state in this paragraph that the agency decided "to cancel the deduction of earnings order, while the paternity dispute was

ongoing". I refer you to item 35 where you stated that Miss Griffin had requested the order be stopped. You have contradicted yourself here. I cite that as incompetence on your part and an example of maladministration in respect of this investigation.

42. You state that the agency "decided to pay you £50.00 as way of redress to apologise for the way it handled your case." This is the agency ADMITTING its maladministration. However, I received NO consolatory payment at this or any other time and given the scale of the maladministration, consider this level of compensation to be insulting.

43. Correct.

44. You suggest that your investigation found no maladministration prior to the paternity dispute. My whole complaint and diary details the maladministration SINCE the paternity dispute was raised. The stress, as detailed in the numerous examples of maladministration I've provided, was as a direct result of my dealings with the agency. You agree that there **was** maladministration, but you cite it as only being minor in respect of delays to the agency responding to me. You seem to have totally ignored all the other examples and evidence I have provided you with. As detailed in 42 above, NO redress has EVER been received. I have provided letters from my fiancées doctor that detail the stress was directly caused by the CSA. It would appear you have simply chosen to ignore this along with the counselling evidence I provided also. I am aghast at how, given the evidence I have supplied, any sane person can suggest the agency was not instrumental in the stress it caused me and my partner.

45. You cite that the agency made a payment to me of £2,137.28 inappropriately. This payment was not inappropriate. The sums I have received **are proper** and I was **entitled** to receive them. Your suggestion that these payments were not proper is not correct. This particular payment was the refund of monies paid directly to the agency for child maintenance. To suggest this is compensation (as the agency did in their letter with the cheque for this amount) or inappropriate is incorrect. I should like it to be noted that you already detailed earlier in your report (No. 19), that this is a refund of monies

paid "through the agency". Therefore, you have made a serious error and contradicted yourself again and I cite this as further example of your maladministration in respect of this investigation. You also go on to refer to a "consolatory payment". As previously detailed, NO payment was received. As no payments in respect of redress have been forthcoming, the agency has NOT provided ANY redress, let alone any that can be referred to as "excessive".

46. The agency did not cooperate. It delayed sending information to you.

47. The investigation was delayed by much longer than seven weeks. It was nearer to double that time.

48. If the "consolatory payment" you refer to is £50.00, I find this considerably below what I would accept as redress for the maladministration that has occurred. As detailed previously: "**action or lack of action [that] caused: serious inconvenience as a result of repeated mistakes**" and "**neglect, inattention, delay, incompetence, ineptitude**" is what I have detailed over 19 A4 pages of my diary. That, along with the other evidence I have submitted, ably demonstrates my claim and I insist, again, that the agency provide SIGNIFICANT redress. I would suggest this redress is of an amount in line with the amount of all monies paid to the PWC and court fees and solicitors costs.

49. I shall be referring this matter to the Parliamentary Ombudsman. The service has, in short, been diabolical. I cannot even begin to comprehend why this report has taken a year to produce. The mistakes and contradictions and inconsistencies within it suggest maladministration and bias to a staggering degree. Not to mention the personal comments made in respect of events outside of the complaint.

50. In light of this report, you can expect any feedback to be somewhat damning. I cannot even begin to understand how you have failed to uphold my complaints.

In summary, the following demonstrates the maladministration and therefore my redress should be as previously requested:

- Report/Investigation was severely delayed by longer than you suggested.
- I was advised to go to court by the CSA. CSA should cover the costs of doing so, as it was on their advice I went to court.
- I was told on two occasions, and have audio recording to prove this; I would get all of the money I paid the PWC back.
- Adam West admitted his incompetence in misquoting/misreading the legislation.
- DOE's were submitted incorrectly causing stress and significant hardship.
- I have cited numerous examples of "**action or lack of action [that] caused: serious inconvenience as a result of repeated mistakes**" and "**neglect, inattention, delay, incompetence, ineptitude**"
- No redress payments have ever been made.
- You and the CSA state "professional fees may only be considered where maladministration has occurred and the engagement of professional help was justified in the pursuit of a child maintenance issue." As this was in pursuit of a child maintenance issue and you concur that the agency has been maladministrative in its dealings with me, I should be refunded appropriately.
- CSA refused to assist me to get the case reviewed when I raised the paternity dispute.
- CSA refused to provide me with list of DNA test centres.
- Your comments in regard to the manner in which the initial DNA test was carried out are inappropriate and outside of your remit in respect of the investigation.
- Errors and contradictions directly within the report (see 11, 13, 35, 36, 41, 45)
- Statements from court hearings that simply did not occur are included – these should be struck from the report as they are not on the court orders and therefore cannot be relied upon as having happened.

- Was informed several times I would get "all costs associated with going to court" back.
- Agency was obstructive and misleading once I notified them of paternity dispute.
- Numerous examples of maladministration as detailed in my original diary notes have been ignored.
- Suggestion that monies paid by me directly to the agency should not have been refunded is incorrect.
- Suggestion, despite evidence being provided, that Miss Griffin had not confirmed direct payments were in lieu of child maintenance.
- Suggested I "waited five years before challenging acceptance" that I was the father when in fact I **discovered** after five years the child in question was not mine.
- Suggestion that monies I have received from the agency were not proper and that I was not entitled to them.
- Statement made to the effect of "I found no evidence you raised a paternity dispute" is negated by evidence provided in which the agency clearly acknowledges the dispute being raised.
- Personal views instead of objectiveness raises questions around bias towards the CSA and against me.
- Evidence provided of stress being directly attributable to the CSA has been ignored.
- Failure of a service provision I was entitled to.
- Numerous delays, in agency responding to my letters, are agreed to have occurred yet you still don't uphold that maladministration occurred despite concurring that it did occur. How can you agree it happened but not uphold my complaint regarding it?

I shall await yours and the Ombudsman's response in respect of my comments here, along with the suggested redress from the CSA. If the redress is not as I have recommended it should be, or near to my expectations, then I shall be forced to pursue the claim through the appropriate court.

Printed in Poland
by Amazon Fulfillment
Poland Sp. z o.o., Wrocław